At the Mercy
of
Strangers

To Helen with appreeciation
& love 70 years after D-Day
Suzanne Loebl

June 6, 2014

At the Mercy of Strangers

of

Strangers

Growing Up On
the Edge of the Holocaust

Suzanne Loebl

Pacifica Press

Manufactured in the United States of America
ISBN 0-935553-23-1

Library of Congress Cataloging-in-Publication Data:

Loebl, Suzanne
    At the mercy of strangers : growing up on the edge of the Holocaust /
Suzanne Loebl
      p.   cm.
    ISBN 0-935553-23-1 (trade hardcover : alk. paper)
    1. Loebl, Suzanne—Childhood and youth. 2. Jewish children in the
Holocaust—Belgium—Biography. 3. Jews, German—Belgium—Biography.
4. Jews—Germany—Hannover—Biography. I. Title.
DS135.B43L64 1997
940.53'18'092—dc21
[B]   97-5154
                                                CIP

To the memory of
Nelly Altorfer,
Mariette and Emile Altorfer,
and for David, always

Acknowledgements

E
ven for a published author it takes special courage to tell her own story. It has taken me years to complete *At the Mercy of Strangers*. The memoir, which incorporates the diary I kept more than fifty years ago, owes its existence to many individuals who through their interest, love, and concern encouraged me not to let the venture die. I want to thank Patricia Argiro, Sivan Bamberger, John Gordon, Jean Guttman, Frank Donnelly, Erica Korody, Herbert Loebl OBE, Lois Lowenstein, Joe Miller, Herbert Morawetz, Howard Smith, Melissa Solomon, Caroline Urvater, and Peter Waldman for their enthusiasm.

I also want to express my heartfelt gratitude to the "Strangers," who in major and minor ways enabled my immediate family to escape the actual flames of the Holocaust: Nelly Altorfer and Jean-Marie Wiame, Dominique and Delphine Bellins, Jean and Jacqueline Corvillain, Mr. and Mrs. J. De Backer and their daughter Eva, René Fuss, Madame "de Groot," Jacqueline and Jean Grosfils, Madame Lebacqz, Suzanne Tamineau, Hein and Bets Vorwinden, and the Vincke family.

Special thanks are due to my husband Ernest for his support and rare patience, to my daughter Judy and my grandchildren, Ana, Naomi, ad Sean, for their keen interest in listening to my, and to my sister Gabrielle, for sharing my life.

Some of the people I want to thank are no longer here. My mom taught me how to tell stories, my dad endowed me with his energy and sense of humor, my son David derived strength from my having survived the Holocaust and also was fascinated by my tales.

I am grateful to the many teachers who in the course of my very checkered education have encouraged me to write—to Hays B. Jacobs and Rick Kondo of the New School for their writing seminars, and to the Columbia University School of Journalism for formalizing all this help in the form of a fellowship.

Warm thanks are also due to Eric Hammel and Pacifica Press for publishing the book, and to Elizabeth von Radics for a superb editing job. And thanks to my long-time friend, Gloria Kamen, for designing the cover.

I want to thank Anne Altorfer for supplying the photographs of her parents and herself, Jacques Wiame for the picture of his father, Dedé Weerens for the pictures of the Hirschland family, the Musée Royal de L'Armée, La Photothèque du Soir, and le Centre de Recherches et d'Etudes Historiques de la Seconde Guerre Mondiale for supplying the photographs of Brussels during the Occupation, and the New York Public Library for making accessible its surprisingly complete collection of books dealing with Belgium during World War II.

Contents

Having to be grateful is hard to cope with, especially if it is for something as fundamental as saving one's own life, so I tried to minimize the danger I and the people who sheltered me faced. In some ways this was easy, because to a certain extent life was drearily mundane. It was precisely the juxtaposition of the daily dullness with the horror of the Holocaust that was characteristic of the crazy time I was living in.

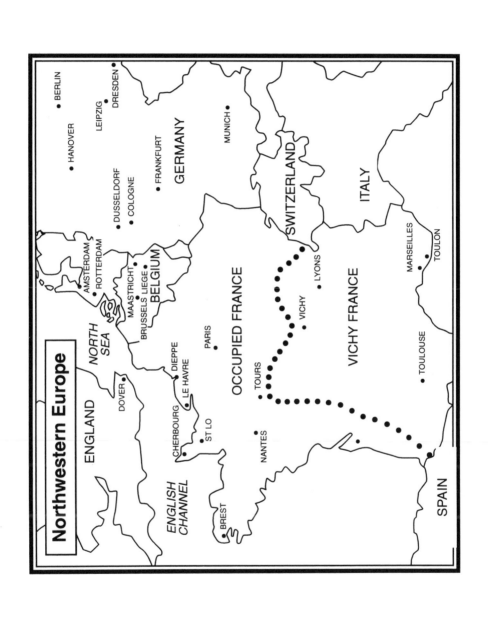

Northwestern Europe

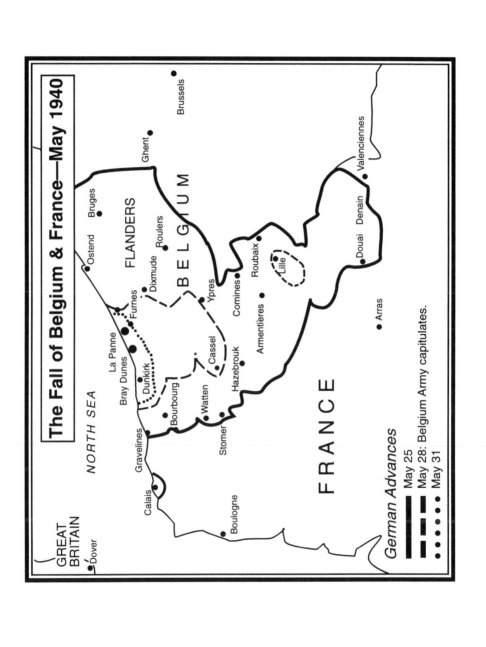

The Fall of Belgium & France—May 1940

GREAT BRITAIN

Dover

NORTH SEA

Calais

Boulogne

Gravelines

Bourbourg

Stomer

Watten

Dunkirk

Bray Dunes

La Panne

Furnes

Cassel

Hazebrouk

Ostend

Bruges

FLANDERS

Dixmude

Roulers

Ghent

Ypres

Comines

BELGIUM

Roubaix

Lille

Armentières

Arras

Brussels

Valenciennes

Denain

Douai

FRANCE

German Advances

—————— May 25
– – – – – May 28: Belgium Army capitulates.
• • • • • May 31

Prologue
The Parade

I hated my smocked, waistless little girl's dress. It was much too babyish for a thirteen year old with budding breasts. All of the other girls in my class wore blouses and skirts or dresses with waists. The dress was suitable for my eight-year-old sister but not for me. So I cinched it with a wide belt, making it much too short.

I hated my hair too. My black curls were still cut in a by then unfashionable short bob. I was impatient and had trouble standing for so long in one place; I was hot. I felt—and was—awkward.

Still, I was proud to be part of the crowd waiting for Leopold III, king of the Belgians. He was to ride down the Boulevard de la Toison d'Or, one of Brussels's imposing thoroughfares. This was my first parade, and I was happy and excited that my class had gone to pay respect to my new ruler. Back in Germany, where I was born, Jews like me were excluded from any public gatherings.

In 1938, when we arrived in Brussels, Adolf Hitler had been in power for as long as I had been able to interact with the outside world. The hate and hostility, the anti-Semitic cartoons in the newspapers, even the condescending kindness extended by some had taught me to hate Germany.

I had been going to this new school for only six weeks and hardly spoke

French, yet I breathed more freely. Even though I was really still an outsider, I felt that Belgium was home, that I belonged.

Our French teacher, Madame Massard, was in charge of my class, the sixth grade, of the Lycée de Forest. She had lined us up along the curb according to size. Because I was short, I stood in the first row.

We waited a long time for the procession to arrive. Finally, we heard a military band, and the handsome young king rode by on a big bay horse. No guards were in sight. We shouted: "Long live the king." The king saluted. Then it was all over. The parade had been a big letdown.

Before dismissing us Madame Massard asked whether we all knew our way. Most of the class did. But I was a newcomer to Brussels; my friend Maria van Weyenberg said she would see that I got home.

The streetcars were jammed with people returning from the parade, so Maria and I decided to walk. We followed the wide outer boulevards that had replaced Brussels's last city wall. Engrossed as we were in ourselves, we were oblivious to the blooming chestnut trees, the other pedestrians, and the traffic.

We chattered as best we could, using hands and gestures whenever necessary. I was learning French fast and tried to be like everybody else. Maria complained that between school and weekly visits to Grandpa, Grandma, and her godmother life was boring. I felt that too much had happened to me in Nazi Germany.

The next thing I remembered was a man pulling me out from under the front end of a truck. For a moment everything was very still. Then I noticed the ring of people that had gathered around Maria, me, and the small truck that had plowed us down as we crossed one of the intersections of the boulevard.

Everybody talked at once. My small store of French left me completely, and I could not make out what people were saying.

The truck driver apparently wanted to drive us home. I refused, having been warned, over and over, not to accept rides from strangers. Somebody offered to phone my mother, a doctor, an ambulance. I started to cry, a little at first, then uncontrollably. My ankle hurt. A man handed me a piece of paper with the license plate number of the truck. I wished that all these people would leave me alone!

Finally Maria managed to extricate us from the crowd. We squeezed aboard a streetcar. I still sobbed.

"What's the matter with her?" the other passengers kept asking Maria. "Leave her alone," Maria said. "She does not speak French."

I felt like a trapped animal. Fortunately, I recognized my stop and got off the streetcar. As soon as I was by myself, I felt a bit better. My terror, however, returned promptly.

What will my mother say? I wondered. I had always been told to watch out when crossing streets! Would my mother fly into one of her terrifying, totally incomprehensible rages? Would she too sob and rant about me adding to my parents' burdens?

I sat on a bench near my house, trying to get up the courage to face my mother. I eventually managed to stop crying. I massaged my red, swollen nose and limped home.

"You look beat," my mom said when she let me in. "I always told you that political parades are no fun. Now you saw for yourself. You must have had too much sun. You should have worn a hat."

I picked at lunch, excusing myself often to go to the bathroom, where I applied cold water to my swelling ankle. I sighed with relief when my mother left to fetch my sister from school.

I was still acting a bit strange when the two of them got back around five o'clock. My mother insisted on knowing what really happened. I confessed.

To my surprise and relief, my mother was not angry, but praised me for not wanting to worry her. She put me to bed with an ice pack and called Dr. Hertz, a German Jewish refugee like ourselves. Before Hitler came to power, Dr. Hertz was a famous professor at the University of Frankfurt. Now his small practice consisted primarily of other refugees.

The swelling in my ankle quickly receded. I returned to school two days later. A medical certificate even gave me a welcome respite from gym, which I hated, because even without the hurt ankle, my performance never met the acceptable standards.

My injury had no lasting physical effects, but crossing streets became a life-long problem. I panic as soon as I see a car appear on the horizon. Sometimes I dash back to the safety of the curb, even when I have almost reached the other side. Sometimes I just freeze.

In spite of such erratic behavior and irrational fear, I always manage to reach the other "shore," relying on traffic lights, joining other pedestrians, seeking out a less daunting path, and, if need be, simply gritting my teeth. I have always been good at solving problems, my own and those of others.

In Germany my parents shielded me as best they could from the gathering Holocaust, but I knew that their life was difficult. I tried not to burden them with my problems and relied on myself. More than that, I quietly assumed many tasks whose execution required judgment and skills far beyond my years. Because my parents wanted me to remain a child, I acted like one, often seeming less competent than I really was. This pattern may account for the mix of nerve and shyness, insight and innocence, assertiveness and docility that helped me navigate through an extraordinary adolescence.

Chapter 1

April Fool's Day, 1938

At first only a handful of Jews took Adolf Hitler seriously and left Germany almost immediately after he came to power during the spring of 1933. In the beginning of his reign, the führer's policies seemed to give official sanction to the chronic, relatively tame anti-Semitism that existed in Germany long before his advent.

My family had lived in Germany for centuries. My father's ancestors came from the small villages that surrounded the town of Bamberg in southern Germany—and so that name became my family's. The men were small-time craftsmen who wove the native wicker into baskets and furniture. During the 1850s my great-grandfather David started to import reeds from Africa and turned the small business into a major enterprise. His firm, David Bamberger, Lichtenfels, (DBL), still existed in 1933. By then wicker was no longer fashionable. My talented uncle Otto, David's grandson, shifted the production to educational toys, and the family enterprise continued to prosper. Whenever I visited my father's hometown, I was allowed to plunder the storerooms. What a delight!

My mother's family also came from southern Germany. In 1761, long before the emancipation of German Jews, an ancestor had been appointed to the court of one of Bavaria's many princes, and he was free. His descendants were tradesmen. Isaak Mayer, one of my maternal great-grandfathers, started out by peddling geese from door to door. By the time he married, he had a store in Frankfurt and he eventually became a wholesaler, importing geese from Hungary. By 1914 he owned Germany's largest cold-storage plant, and during World War I he stored meat for the army of the kaiser.

My other maternal great-grandfather, Emanuel Schwarzhaupt, also started out as an itinerant salesman. When he died his six sons owned a chain of successful clothing stores in such well-known towns as Nuremberg, Regensburg, and Munich. The one in Nuremberg was headed by my grandfather Joseph and his brother Heinrich.

The material comfort of many German Jews was recent. Even though Jews had lived in Germany since Roman times, they had never been fully accepted. For most of their two-thousand-year-long history, they could not own land, attend universities, hold public office, serve in the armed forces, or live where they pleased. Though Jews contributed to Germany's culture and economic well-being, their lives were punctuated by discrimination, riots, and pogroms.

In 1925, when I was born, these problems seemed part of the past. Two generations earlier, when my grandfather Joseph was born in 1871, discrimination was abolished throughout Germany, and the Jews attained full equality. Germany prospered, as did many German Jews, including my family.

Emancipation created new problems, however. Some Jews abandoned Judaism altogether and had themselves baptized. Others remained Jews but no longer practiced their religion. Others continued to adhere closely to Jewish tradition, celebrating the holidays and maintaining kosher homes.

Discrimination, unfortunately, never vanishes with the stroke of a pen. Social and professional barriers were slow to crumble. My parents' and grandparents' friends were mostly Jewish. Jews were not admitted to the officer corps of the German army and held few teaching jobs and government appointments.

Both my mother's and my father's families were extremely loyal, patriotic Germans. My father and his three brothers fought in World War I with valor. My father was even decorated. Two of my mother's three male cousins were among the twelve thousand Jews killed in the course of that war.

Long before emancipation was official, the German Jews loved German culture. Splendid German art embellished my house, and the music of Bach and Beethoven filled the air. Christmas with its pomp, candles, and cookies was my mother's favorite holiday. My parents felt that any remaining prejudices would vanish with time. German Jews felt secure, and they could not believe that their compatriots would tolerate Hitler for long.

They were wrong. Hitler lasted, and the century-long anti-Semitism was so deeply embedded in the minds of many Germans that it readily erupted when stimulated by the Nazis.

I was eight years old when the Nazis came to power, and my sister was three. We understood none of all that, but reacted to the prevailing mixed signals. One day my sister reported that she had had a nightmare in which she was chased by a Jew. I knew that I was Jewish, but did not really understand what it meant. We did not go to church, but then we did not go to a synagogue either. It was most confusing!

I was a rather solitary child, but when I entered school I suddenly had a best friend and was elated. Within the year Gerda's family left for Switzerland and I never saw her again. Even now, sixty-five years later, I still miss her. When I asked my mom why Gerda left, she mumbled something about "being cautious" and "being rich." I sensed that my parents did not want to be asked any questions about what was happening in Germany.

The Germans love law and order. From the time they assumed power, the Nazis passed anti-Jewish decrees that defined the social and economic relationships between Germans and Jews. The first laws, whose purpose was to prevent "the sullying of German blood," required defining who was Jewish and who wasn't. There were full Jews, like me, who had four Jewish grandparents, and half Jews and even quarter Jews. Non-Jews could no longer marry Jews.

Jewish-owned stores had to identify themselves as such. Jewish lawyers were forbidden to practice law, Jewish medical students could not graduate from the University, and newspapers had to fire their Jewish editors. Public schools refused to admit Jewish pupils. Gentile doctors refused to treat Jewish patients. Jews could no longer employ Gentile girls as household help.

To me these new rules made no sense. We had gone to the same restaurants and hotels as Gentiles for as long as I remembered. Now there were signs saying, "Jews Unwelcome." Anna, our cook, who had worked for us for many years, was part of the family. I wondered why she had to leave us now. Dr. Huneus, my pediatrician, had taken care of me since birth. Now he refused to come when I was ill.

Not all Germans wanted to comply with these insane measures. Anna told my mother that she planned to write to Hitler, asking for permission to stay with us. Some Gentile friends continued to visit. But the Nazis used the carrot-and-the-stick principle. The faithful were rewarded; those who did not comply were punished.

My mother impressed upon me to be good, polite, and invisible. I knew that my parents had many worries. I did not wish to add to their distress, so I did as I was told.

I had graduated from the local elementary school, and it was difficult to find a middle school willing to enroll a ten-year-old Jewish child. Finally the Waldorf School, located at the other end of town, accepted me. My mother stressed that I had to be grateful that the school took me.

I wish that my mother had sent me to the Jewish school. There I would have been with children who shared my problems. My parents, however, felt so non-Jewish that they were more comfortable with a German school.

The Waldorf schools are based on a Christianized form of theosophy developed by Rudolf Steiner. Anthroposophy, as it is called, stresses the goodness of man, spirituality, and the healing power of nature. Its philosophy was the complete opposite of National Socialism—so much so that the Nazis eventually closed the schools.

When I joined the class, the teachers and students were accepting, and I mostly enjoyed my new school. There was only one other Jewish child in my class, Ruth-Iris Freudenthal, whom I guiltily disliked because I considered her too meek. I did stick up for her, though. I made friends with some of the other children, a few of whom were even brave enough to invite me to their homes. Still I was an outsider. I could not join the BDM (Bund Deutscher Mädchen), the female arm of the Hitler Youth. I was careful to duck Grete Stinnis, a dyed-in-the wool Nazi, who reported to the local authorities anyone who was too nice to me or Ruth-Iris.

Ruth-Iris and I were exempted from the weekly lessons on National Socialist theory, but we took religion. Here I learned all about Jesus and his disciples and was awed by his goodness, his kindness, and his wisdom of turning the other cheek when wronged.

One of my principal sources of information about Jews was the *Stürmer,* an anti-Semitic rag posted in a glass box, prominently displayed at my streetcar stop. The pages of the *Stürmer,* published by one of Hitler's close associates, were filled with cartoons depicting Jews with hooked noses, big teeth, curly black hair, and money-grubbing habits. I remember the cartoon of a newborn clutching a diamond ring, stolen from the doctor assisting his mother during his birth. Was I like these Jews? Yes, I did have a big nose, black curly hair, and more money than the other children in my class.

Slowly, I discovered more facts about the mysterious tribe to which I belonged. When I was eleven, the Jewish community in Hanover insisted that the children of all members in good standing attend Hebrew school. I learned about my fair, angry God, who believed in justice and retribution: "An eye for an eye," he said. This too made sense. I went to Hebrew school once a week, enjoyed the company of my fellow students, and felt at home, even though my mother thought that it was a waste of time. On the High Holidays, my father and I even started going to the temple.

My double religious instruction added to my confusion. Could both religions be correct? To cover all my bases, I started addressing my nightly prayers to: "Dear God and Dear Jesus Christ."

In many respects my childhood was normal and happy. My father continued to work hard at the small chemical factory he had founded. To his staff he still was the highly respected, beloved boss.

We visited with my mother's family in Frankfurt. My grandparents spoiled me; my aunt Erna treated me like a grown-up. We went out to lunch, and she even bought me special soap and moisturizing cream for my skin. I fell in love with her son, my cousin Ernest.

Each summer I spent some time in Lichtenfels, my father's hometown. My grandparents had died before I was born, but family holidays and vacations were spent in my aunt Jetta's house. We were ten cousins, close enough in age to be real pals. We hiked in the spectacular countryside, swam, and explored ruined castles and historic churches.

Not that Lichtenfels was free of anti-Semitism. One summer Jews were banned from swimming in the river Main—a body of water we cousins considered our own. The next year we were asked not to attend the annual fair—one of the highlights of the vacation. But because there were so many of us, we made our own parties, and these summers are my happiest memories of Germany.

There were also other family vacations—trips to Switzerland and Italy. There was my beloved Marie, who had worked for my parents since I was born and had retired when I was five. Because she was old, she was allowed to work for Jews and came back to help my mother manage her immense house. And then there was my little sister.

I still remember the day Gaby was born. I was five at the time and resented being dethroned from my only-child status. I was jealous of the attention she received, but already I must have possessed the ability to make the best out of the inevitable. I turned Gaby into my helpmate and ally, and jointly we coped with our over-busy, preoccupied parents.

In spite of my parents' efforts, hate and Jew-baiting filtered through. Once as Gaby and I and Peter, our fox terrier, were ambling down the street, a band of boys started to materialize with sticks. They yelled, "Jew-bastards," and we started running, Peter close on our heels.

"Leave the dog alone," the ringleader shouted. "It is not his fault."

It was not only children who baited the Jews, however. Many anti-Semitic acts were perpetrated by ordinary grown-ups. Once when I went to the local swimming pool, a man simply asked for my last name. "Bamberger," I said. Concluding that this was a Jewish name, he told me to get dressed and go home.

Another time, while on an overnight school trip, Ruth-Iris and I were abruptly asked to leave the small inn at which my mother had arranged shelter, while the rest of the class stayed at the youth hostel: One of the other guests at the inn refused "to sleep under the same roof with Jews." Because he was a powerful SS officer, the innkeeper, who had agreed to put us up even though he knew we were Jewish, thought it prudent to comply. I had to call my parents, who came to fetch us home in the middle of the night.

But it was the unknown, unspoken threats that were more scary than anything that actually happened to me. I knew that my uncle Otto had been arrested and sent to a prison. He was released, but the strain had been so severe that he died a few months later. Other people disappeared mysteriously.

I started to train myself to be more courageous. In winter, night fell early in Hanover, so by the time I got back from school, the stars were out. Sometimes, instead of going straight home along the well-lit street, I entered the forest that bordered it.

The dark, naked limbs of the trees shook. The wind whistled through the branches. It was ice-cold and pitch dark. I would stand stock still and will myself to be calm. I was afraid and elated. After a few extremely long minutes, I would leave the woods and return to my warm, cheery house.

♦

Once anti-Semitism had been properly fanned, the Nazis instituted numerous laws designed to impoverish the Jewish community. Employees were fired, pensions were curtailed, and fines and special taxes were levied. Eventually, Jewish businesses were taken over by Germans.

These measures ruined some of my parents' friends. I remember the evening my formerly wealthy "uncle" Herman Scheiberg came to see my parents. Now poor and totally distraught, he reluctantly accepted some money from my parents. A few weeks later, he commited suicide. His wife, my cheerful and exuberant "aunt" Paula, came to see us. She wore black and cried all evening, trying to find some solace. A few weeks later, she too committed suicide.

By 1935 many of Germany's 600,000 Jews, including my parents, realized that they had to leave their native land, but it was no easy task to find a country willing to accept refugees. The red tape involved in obtaining immigration visas to a new country and exit visas from Germany was mindboggling. No country wanted poor Jews, although some were willing to accept wealthy immigrants or those who would make a positive contribution to the economy.

Though Germany was delighted to get rid of its Jews, the Nazis wanted to hang on to their material possessions. These, the authorities claimed, rightfully belonged to Germany. From 1933 on, the Nazis evolved a continuously escalating set of regulations governing the export of money, household goods, jewelry, precious metals, and other items. In typical Teutonic fashion the rules specified that gold used for wedding bands and to fix teeth did not have to be turned in. Bank accounts were frozen, and Jewish property could not be sold on the open market. Germans bought Jewish businesses for a fraction of their actual value. And those Jews lucky enough to leave were taxed for "fleeing" the German Reich.

My family was luckier than most. My father owned his business, and thus could not be fired. Moreover, because his small chemical plant exported food preservatives and pharmaceuticals to other European countries, he had contacts abroad. His clients in Holland, Belgium, and Spain were willing to sponsor him because his enterprise would make a valuable economic contribution to the local economy.

My father loved Spain and always looked forward to his yearly business trip there. His major clients in the Spanish olive industry assured him of their continued patronage, should he relocate. Spain was therefore my parents' first choice. They proudly looked at my dark hair and greenish eyes and concluded that I looked Spanish enough to blend in. My parents applied for the necessary immigration papers—and waited.

During his student days at the University of Würzburg in Germany, my father had become friends with Fritz Rothschild, another Jew. Their friendship outlasted their student days, and Fritz became a well-to-do lawyer. He and his wife, Hertha, were childless and became our doting "aunt and uncle."

After the Nazis closed his practice, Fritz and my father became business partners. They were to establish a small chemical factory abroad, Fritz providing the capital, Hertha the secretarial help, and my father the technical expertise and clients.

In 1935 Fritz and Hertha set out for Spain. They opened a small office in Barcelona. We were to follow a year later. Long before my family got the necessary papers to join them, however, Spain became embroiled in its bloody civil war between the forces supporting Francisco Franco—a Fascist like Mussolini and Hitler—and the Loyalists backed by liberals and Communists. This civil war, which many historians now consider the dress rehearsal for World War II, plunged Spain into total disarray. This was neither the time nor place to start a new business, so Fritz and Hertha left Barcelona.

Italy was the next country in which Fritz Rothschild and my father tried to become established. Mussolini, called Il Duce, had ruled Italy since 1922. When someone asked my parents if they were worried about the possibility of Il Duce instituting anti-Semitic measures, they replied with great conviction: "Mussolini would never persecute the Jews." Indeed, during the early part of his reign, many Italian Jews had joined the Fascist Party. In 1936 after Hitler and Mussolini proclaimed the Rome-Berlin Axis, the bond between the two countries tightened.

Fritz and Hertha opened a small office in Milan, and my father joined them there in 1937. Soon thereafter Il Duce complied with Hitler's anti-Semitic policies, so Italy clearly was not the place to be.

Fortunately, my parents and the Rothschilds had also applied for Belgian immigration papers. To survey the country, my parents had driven to Brussels in 1936. It so happened that just as they crossed the border, both the German and the Belgian armies had maneuvers. Skeptically, my mother asked my father whether he truthfully believed that the Belgian army would be able to defend us against the obviously more powerfully armed German hoodlums.

In spite of my mother's well-grounded fears, Fritz and Hertha relocated to Brussels in late 1937. My father followed soon thereafter. Again the three founded a small chemical factory. They christened the enterprise La Synthèse, (French for *synthesis*), a name that not only referred to a well-known chemical process but also symbolized my father's hope of economically providing for his family.

My mother, my eight-year-old sister, and I stayed on for a little while in Hanover. My mother was packing up our complex household, selling books, giving plants to friends and neighbors, and having some of our massive German furniture rebuilt so that it would fit into a small apartment.

Our emigration papers allowed us to take our furniture and clothes. My father was even granted permission to export laboratory equipment. My mother converted as much of our now mostly useless money as she dared into material possessions: clothes, new kitchen equipment, even some works of art. My father bought the best laboratory equipment available, including some solid platinum ware.

One important reason for our tarrying in Germany was family—my maternal grandparents and my great-grandmother. My mother feared that we might never see them again, and she wanted my sister and me to visit for a long time with Opa, Oma, and Oma Mayer in Frankfurt.

My grandfather was more deeply upset by the political events than anybody else I knew. He was both a loyal German and the only member of my immediate family who was still a devout Jew. He listened to his rabbi, attended synagogue, and prayed. When we visited he blessed me and my sister each morning in Hebrew:

May the Lord keep you and protect you . . .
May his light shine upon you . . .

Opa was a very upright and God-fearing man. He suspected that some relatives, even his wife and daughters, were smuggling money and jewelry out of Germany. He begged to be kept uninformed of these activities, because he knew that he would tell the truth if questioned under oath. Opa realized that we were about to emigrate to Belgium, but he could not bear the thought of us leaving. So Gaby and I were instructed not to talk about it with him. I hated taking part in this cover-up and felt guilty when he came into our room to kiss us good-night, saying that he knew we would leave him soon.

Although the exact date of our departure for Brussels was not fixed, during March 1938 the Gestapo inquired about my mother's whereabouts. She had been an active member of a now defunct organization promoting international peace and freedom. This made her vulnerable to arrest. The official inquiry scared my mother, and she decided that we would leave Germany at once.

My mother always wanted to take an airplane. When she was a teenager in Nurnberg, she repeatedly saved money for a sight-seeing flight. This was during the skyrocketing German inflation of 1919. Whenever she went to pay for her airplane ride, the price of the ticket had increased beyond her means. Because to us German money was once more worthless, we decided to fly to Belgium on April first—April Fools' Day.

We sneaked down the back stairs of my grandparents' house with our luggage so as not to say good-bye to Opa. My heart was tight about leaving the dear, old man. It was early in the morning, though our plane was scheduled for the afternoon. That day Hitler had scheduled a triumphant entry into Frankfurt to celebrate his recent annexation of Austria. We feared that the road to the airport might be closed to civilian traffic.

In 1938 it was a major event to take a plane. I was sorry that I could not brag about it to my class in Hanover. As the plane lifted off, I watched Frankfurt becoming smaller and smaller. I saw the old cathedral whose spire my mother and I had often climbed. From there we had looked down on Frankfurt's famous Old City. Medieval houses ringed an open square—the Roemer, so-called because it dated back to Roman times when the city was already an important trading post. Then as now there was a market on the Roemer; colorful umbrellas shielded the stalls from sun and rain. After the climb up the tower, my mother and I would stop at a stand to eat a hot sausage with mustard on a bun. This snack was, of course, the original Frankfurter—the hot dog.

Soon our plane left Frankfurt behind. We flew above the clouds that the setting sun had turned a deep orange. I felt no regret about leaving my hostile native land.

My mother had telegraphed my father, informing him of our arrival. Since this was April first, he believed it to be one of his wife's April Fools'

Day pranks. Each April our house was booby-trapped with mustard-spiked pastry or pajamas whose legs had been sewn closed. My parents sent each other on fool's errands or bogus dates. Vati had no intention of going to the airport to fetch us. Fortunately, Uncle Fritz insisted, and we were duly met by the two men.

We spent our first night in Brussels in what I considered a fancy hotel. Actually, the still-existing Hotel Central is located in the commercial, seedy part of town. Because we had not really had any food since breakfast, we went out to eat even though it was way past our usual bedtime.

Bright lights lit the boulevards of my new hometown. People filled the glass-enclosed terraces of the many cafes. Uncle Fritz shepherded us to a fashionable ice-cream parlor. The Coupe Glacée offered an unbelievable selection of flavors and unfamiliar ice-cream concoctions: hot-fudge sundaes, parfaits, *coupe aux marrons,* and banana splits. Uncle Fritz, who loved to spoil us, said that we could order whatever we liked.

My father had sublet quarters from a barber, and we joined him there until our furniture arrived. Long before it came, I was back in school.

Chapter 2

New Roots

In Brussels my mother's first task was to find a school for my sister and me. A few weeks after our arrival, we visited the principal of the Lycée de Forest, the high school serving my neighborhood. With her hair tightly pulled in a bun and her steel gray eyes, Vera Tordeur, the principal of the school, looked forbidding. She placed me, strictly according to my age, in the sixth—the lowest—grade of the lycée. Even though she had been kind and courteous, Madame Tordeur terrified me. I would tremble each time she entered my classroom, expecting her to expel me from the school. My sister was registered at Forest's elementary school, located around the corner from the lycée. The schools were about a mile from our new apartment, a distance Gaby and I covered four times a day.

I arrived in the schoolyard of my new school the following Monday. The bell rang. A teacher shouted: "Silence, line up." Three hundred girls, two abreast, lined up by class. I had identified my class and marched with it to our classroom. I was scared and unhappy.

In class Madame Massard welcomed me and explained that I was a Jewish refugee from Germany. Then she asked whether anyone was willing to help me navigate through the early, difficult months. Maria van Weyenberg volunteered, so I was told to sit next to her.

I looked around. Most of my fellow students seemed more grown-up than I was. Many had permanents and breasts. Though I was self-conscious, I also sensed that the other kids looked at me with well-meaning curiosity.

Schools in Belgium are divided into six years of elementary school, six years of high school (the lycée for girls, the athenée for boys), followed by professional or university-level schools. In 1938 the high schools were subdivided into two distinct courses of study: the Latines, emphasizing classical education, including Latin and Greek, and the Moderne, emphasizing modern languages and practical skills. Because Latin and Greek were prerequisites for admission to the university, this difference somewhat segregated the student body. Only upper- and middle-class parents expected their children to continue their studies beyond age eighteen.

Belgium's education standards were high, and few parents found it necessary to send their children to private school. The student body of the Lycée de Forêt represented a cross-section of Brussels's population.

Because I arrived in April, I entered the sixème Moderne class toward the end of the school year. This increased my bewilderment. In spite of many private lessons, I hardly spoke any French. I stammered and stuttered when I was asked a question. The teachers sounded as if they spoke gibberish. It was a long two months until I comprehended something as simple as the homework assignments. Total immersion, however, did wonders for my French. When I finally understood enough French to laugh with the other girls, I knew that I would make it.

Everybody took school very seriously. Our curriculum was rigorous. The school day was longer than it had been in Germany: 8 A.M. to 12 P.M. and 2 to 5 P.M., with a half day on Saturday. There was lots of homework to boot.

In spite of all that hard work, I loved my school. Its paternalistic and authoritarian atmosphere forged a strong spirit of allegiance among the students. The class was one. Snitching was unpardonable. It was the first time in my life that my peers considered me an equal—or almost. I knew that they thought me a bit odd. Still, as my French continued to improve, I felt at home at the Lycée de Forest, more so than in any school before or since. Eventually, the class elected me class secretary. It was a backhanded compliment, bestowed because the class thought that having to take care of the affairs of the twenty pupils might teach me to become more organized and orderly. I was an excellent class secretary, and though I did not become neater, the honor did a lot for my self-esteem.

Not everyone in class liked me. There were several other Jewish children. Ida Kaminsky and Paula Blum had been born in Belgium, but their parents had come from Poland. In Germany, there often had been tension between newly arrived Eastern European Jews and those born there. Many of the German Jews, who were assimilated, greeted their more Orthodox brethren with disdain and contempt. By being openly hostile, Ida and Paula were paying me back for some of these slights.

Grete Wiener, a German Jewish refugee like me, maintained her distance because her mother told her "to integrate" and not mix with other refugees. Another enemy was Nina de Tchernic, whose aristocratic Russian family had to leave Russia after the Soviets came to power in 1917. Nina was imbued with the traditional anti-Semitism of her czarist ancestors.

Some of the teachers also were ambivalent and even downright hostile. I never figured out whether they minded my being German or my being Jewish. Their animosity was not always without cause. I was at odds with Madame Scholarts, who taught Flemish (her native tongue), English, and German. Her German was atrocious, and I regularly raised my hand in class to correct her mistakes. During the other language classes she taught, Madame Scholarts took her revenge; I almost flunked Flemish and English.

Having grown up in a different culture, I found many aspects of my new environment puzzling. This was my first all-girl school. I was a tomboy by nature and always related more easily to the boys than the girls. I could not fathom why my Belgian schoolmates believed that boys belonged to an entirely different species from girls. At that time, teenagers were strictly segregated according to sex, and girls were chaperoned. Once Madame Massard took Rosette, the undisputed beauty of the class, to task, because she had seen her coming out of a park "alone" with a boy.

I ran afoul of the home economics teacher, who demonstrated how to cook meat. She had failed to wash it, as I had seen our cook do in Germany. I raised my hand, questioning her technique. The teacher's response was so scathing that I have not washed a piece of meat since. This taught me to shut up when confronted by different customs or by an unreasonably righteous person in a position of authority.

Other people welcomed my family. There was Madame De Backer, my sister's teacher and our neighbor, who shepherded Gaby to and from school when I couldn't. There were other refugees who had preceded us by months or years and now helped us get settled. There was Mr. Clercq, a teacher and the father of my friend Viviane, who sometimes picked the two of us up at school. Mr. Clercq talked to me as though I was an intelligent grown-up. He said that only those who are too stupid to imagine danger are never scared. Being afraid, he said, did not necessarily turn you into a coward, it simply made you evaluate the risks you took more carefully. How often I would remember this conversation.

I was never much of a student. After the great initial challenge of learning French and catching up with the schoolwork, I was again content with passing grades, in all subjects but one: history. This course, taught by Dr. Denise Feytmans, a handsome, elegant young woman, was pure magic.

When Mademoiselle Feytmans lectured, the classroom vanished. I was transported to the agora in Athens, listening to Socrates debate philosophy with his pupils. I conquered Asia with Alexander the Great, voted with the Senate in Rome, and marched down the Italian peninsula with Hanibal and his elephants. I was clearly Mademoiselle Feytmans's star pupil; she called on me to recite the lesson whenever the other students performed unsatisfactorily.

My grade in that class was as high as it could be: an almost unattainable 10. I knew that if one day I could study what I really loved, it would be history. But in 1938 I knew that this was only a dream.

I had few social contacts with my classmates outside school, but visited back and forth with the children of other refugees. No longer an outcast, I could join youth groups. I became a proud member of the Girl Scouts. My troop was appropriately called *Joy*. Each girl was given an animal name as a "totem." Mine was Enterprising Raven. I liked the *enterprising* portion of the totem but resented being likened to an ugly raven.

My troop met once or twice a week. I laboriously learned the Morse code, tying knots, and providing first aid. I was ambitious, hardworking, capable, and trustworthy. Yet, being a newcomer and a refugee, I felt that I was not entitled to assume any kind of leadership role. I remained a simple scout. Indeed, with rare exceptions, such shyness and false modesty have plagued me my entire life. I have always been more comfortable being "the power behind the throne" than being officially in charge.

I had been so much of an outsider in Germany that I acclimatized rapidly to my new country. I wanted to belong and felt patriotic and at ease.

By habit or conditioning, Belgians are usually in sympathy with the oppressed. Belgium's own long enslavement had imbued the entire population with a dislike and contempt for authority. My new countrymen took great pleasure in evading bureaucracy. These skills would play a crucial role in saving Jewish lives.

In 1831, in the wake of the French Revolution, Belgium had been cobbled together from the French-speaking Walloons and the Dutch-speaking Flemings. Almost from the beginning, there were tensions between these two population groups.

Since its founding, the country had been governed by an elected parliament and a king. The Belgian kings had been well liked and successful. The first Leopold, the favorite uncle of Queen Victoria of Britain, consolidated the fledgling state. The second Leopold acquired the huge Belgian Congo. His successor, Albert I, who ruled during the First World War, was the country's much beloved soldier-king. His son, Leopold III, whom I had watched parading down the Toison d'Or, was only the fourth ruler of Belgium.

The Belgians treasured their new sovereignty. The first line of their national anthem—*After centuries and centuries of bondage, the Belgian, emerging from his tomb*—commemorates the country's long struggle for freedom. Being tightly wedged between France and Germany, Belgium often served as a battleground for these traditional enemies.

In 1914, at the beginning of World War I, the Germans overran Belgium and stayed until the end of the war in November 1918. Their occupation was brutal. Acts of sabotage, real or alleged, were severely punished. In the provincial town of Dinant, for example, the Germans retaliated against an act of civilian disobedience by executing every tenth male regardless of age. On the appointed day, the Germans shot old and middle-aged men, teenage boys, children, and even infants. Dinant commemorated the event by erecting a monument consisting of an immense raised hand, swearing eternal vengeance. In the rest of Belgium, streets and hospitals were named for World War I heroes.

Administratively, the town of Brussels was divided into about twelve boroughs, each of which had a lot of autonomy. We had rented an apartment in the Commune de Forest. Compared to the large house we had occupied in Hanover, it was small—but cozy. It comfortably accommodated our massive German furniture: the oak dining-room set, the living room's immense black velvet armchairs, six glass-fronted bookcases, and my parents' Bauhaus bedroom set.

It took some time for us to learn to take care of ourselves. In Germany we had had help who shopped, cooked, cleaned, washed, ironed, mended, and even looked after the children. Now my mother had a hard time coping with all the chores, even though we employed a cleaning woman. My father, Gaby, and I were given various jobs such as washing the dishes, cleaning the shoes, making beds, preparing dinner, or dusting. There were many arguments, because, being messy by nature, I usually failed to perform up to the expected standards. My mother claimed that she could not live with me and threatened to send me away to a boarding school. She said that she would make the tuition by cleaning house for others. Looking back I can't fathom how I believed these threats, but at the time I took them to heart and was upset about letting my mother down.

My parents talked a lot about money. Although my father's little chemical factory was successful, it was still not producing any income, and we lived off the money my parents had been able to transfer or smuggle out of Germany.

We had never worried about money before, but now we economized. Even though the Nazis had granted my father permission to export our car—a new Opel—my parents felt that operating it was beyond our means. My father, an avid driver, reluctantly stored his pride and joy in a garage at his factory.

My mother looked for food specials and dyed her own hair. She questioned the money I needed to go on an overnight school trip and to buy my Girl Scout uniform. She said that I could have one or the other. I opted for the uniform. When I told the teacher that I could not go on the school trip, she offered a subsidy. I was much too proud to accept such a handout and reluctantly agreed to go on the trip in lieu of acquiring my uniform. The day of the trip I feigned a violent earache. Though she suspected foul play, my mother let me stay home. My gamble paid off. The school returned the trip money, and I could buy my second-hand Girl Scout uniform. I proudly wore the painfully acquired garment and the plaid neckerchief that identified my troop.

We made many friends among Brussels's other German Jewish refugees. Like us, most had no close relatives in Belgium, and we rapidly became each other's family. On Sundays adults and children explored the Belgian country-side and picnicked in the woods surrounding Brussels.

The grown-ups visited with each other most evenings. There always was coffee and cake. Like my mother, many of the women kept their own houses for the first time in their lives. They were proud of their baking and exchanged recipes. The men talked about the difficulty of making a living in a new and foreign country.

Everybody glumly discussed the latest political news. Even though we had escaped, we were intensely involved in what was happening in Germany. My grandparents, other relatives, and many friends were all stuck "back home." News about the increasing persecution of the Jews was worrisome.

Having gathered strength from his success with the bloodless annexation of Austria in the spring of 1938, Hitler pretended that the Germans living in the Czech Sudetenland needed his protection. Czechoslovakia, however, had a treaty with France, guaranteeing its integrity. Since France had a treaty with Britain, the violation of Czech territory might precipitate a world war. During the summer of 1938, Britain's prime minister, Neville Chamberlain, went on what can only be described as a pilgrimage to see Hitler in Germany.

On September 29, 1938, at a summit meeting in Munich, Hitler, Chamberlain, Mussolini, and Prime Minister Edouard Daladier of France, signed an agreement. Germany exacted annexation of the Sudetenland, a ten-thousand-square-mile territory containing all the Czech border fortifications, as a price for peace. The agreement left Czechoslovakia completely unprotected.

The four signatories of the Munich Pact guaranteed the survival of what remained of the Czech state. Its independence, however, lasted only another five months, until March 1939, when the Germans occupied all of Czechoslovakia. The agreement reached at the summit meeting was a farce. Even today, some sixty years later, *Munich* is synonymous with futile appeasement.

In Germany anti-Jewish measures multiplied. In October 1938 the Nazis decreed that Jewish passports had to be stamped with a large *J*, and that every Jew had to have a Jewish first name.

Anxiety escalated. Jews realized that they must leave Germany. Any doubt about their future evaporated during the night of November 9-10, 1938:

Kristallnacht. Using a minor pretext, Nazi hoodlums, now joined by "ordinary citizens," went on a rampage, smashing windows, and burning and looting Jewish stores, homes, and synagogues. That night the mob ransacked 7,500 Jewish stores, torched 1,200 synagogues, and sent 35,000 Jewish men to concentration camps. The name *Kristallnacht* (the night of the broken glass) commemorates the millions of glass shards that littered Germany's streets.

There was no place for most German, Austrian, and Czech Jews to go. Long lines formed outside all consulates. A rigid quota controlled visas to the United States, the safe haven everybody wanted to reach. This quota was based on the ethnic mix of the U.S. population in 1920. It turned out that the comparatively large German and Austrian quotas (27,300) had not been filled during the previous five years, when many European Jews could have reached its shores. In the light of the European debacle, the United States promised to do better. Still, visas were issued at a snail's pace. The wait for Jews born in Poland was practically eternal.

Anyone applying for a U.S. visa was issued a quota number, indicating the approximate date at which a visa might be issued. When the date finally arrived, an American consul interviewed the applicant and decided whether to grant a visa. Causes for refusal were manifold and did not have to be explained. No one with a questionable political background, physical or mental disease, or likely to become a financial burden to the United States received a visa. Special U.S. visas, sponsored by Eleanor Roosevelt, were granted to scholars, artists, or the politically vulnerable.

Some countries, such as Britain, offered long transit visas to persons with reasonable U.S. quota numbers. Other countries accepted a few rich immigrants or those with unusually useful skills. Small South American countries such as Cuba, the Dominican Republic, Venezuela, Honduras, and Ecuador issued a few visas. Some of these were genuine; others, bought from shady middlemen or greedy consular employees, were bogus. Larger South American countries—Argentina, Brazil, Chile, and Mexico—accepted a total of 85,000 Jews. Shanghai was the only place in the world without a quota; it sheltered 10,000 Jews. About 55,000 Jews were able to reach Palestine—the future Israel—then a British mandate.

The mail we received from family and friends was censored, but we could feel the fear and despair between the lines. Some of the letters were happy: "We are leaving for Shanghai and even can take Grandma," or "Our visas for Palestine arrived."

Sometimes we even had unexpected visitors. My aunt Erna and cousin
Edith arrived at our house shortly after Kristallnacht. They had received
their British visas and were passing through Brussels on their way to
England. When I listened to their account of the pogrom, I thanked my
lucky stars that I lived in Brussels.

My father's brother Anton and his family embarked in Rotterdam,
Holland, for America. A distant uncle living in Cleveland, Gustave
Bamberger, had provided the affidavits. Anton's family brought fresh news
from Hanover. Ruth-Iris and her family were still in town, and some of the
girls in my old class had been severely chastised for associating with her.

The cunning and chicanery involved in obtaining the correct papers for
emigration and immigration were bizarre, and the outcome of the machina-
tions was iffy. For months my mother tried to obtain Belgian visas for my
grandparents. In the end the permission was refused. Luck and resourceful-
ness were important. Some people remembered long-forgotten friends and
relatives; others got hold of a New York telephone book and wrote to anyone bearing their family name. They hoped that the unknown addressees
were relatives or sympathetic enough to provide the affidavit necessary for a
U.S. visa application.

After Kristallnacht my mother received a letter from Carrie Van Biema,
her former art teacher, writing from her haven in Holland: "My mother and
my sister Margaret are still in Hanover," Carrie wrote. "I vaguely remember
that forty years ago, in Brussels, I danced with a cousin by the name of
Seligman. I heard that he became a high officer in the Belgian army. Could
you look him up and plead for my mother and sister?"

My mother located the now-retired General Seligman, one of only three
Jewish high military officers in the Belgian army. The short old man, sporting a big mustache and carrying a huge umbrella, came to our house one
afternoon. He bristled when my mother called him "Your Excellency," saying that the Belgian army was not the German army. Addressing him as
"mon Général" would do. The general pulled some strings, and a few months
later his heretofore unknown cousins arrived.

The Van Biemas became his and our good and loyal friends. Margaret,
a fifty-year-old music teacher, even fell in love with the general. Incredibly
romantic Margaret and her mother liked to give musical teas on Sunday
afternoons. Mother Van Biema played the piano, and Margaret sang of the

pain of unrequited love. The General never became romantically involved with his cousin, but eventually the two shared quarters, and he was heartbroken when Margaret died twenty years later.

As German anti-Semitism escalated, several organizations began rescuing the children. Belgium and England issued a limited number of visas for minors. These children, with name tags around their necks, as if they were going to camp, kissed their parents good-bye, often forever. They left Germany in a sealed train via Kindertransport (children's convoy). Some of these children joined relatives; others were placed with foster families.

My parents offered to take seventeen-year-old Herbert Sterner, the only son of my mother's not-too-beloved cousin Else. Both my mother, who had wanted a son, and I, who wanted an older brother, were looking forward to Herbert's arrival.

Herbert was hardly the brother I dreamt of. He lisped badly. His wavy black hair was slicked down with pomade. An acrid smell attested that he seldom washed. This drove Vati to distraction. Herbert also was sloppy and talked back to my father. Within weeks after Herbert's arrival, the relative peace of my family was shattered.

Herbert's favorite words were *"bei uns . . . ,"* implying that "at home" things were different, and by implication, better. The phrase applied to the food, the superiority of his old school, the loving care of his parents and grandmother, and, most of all, the glory of the family's century-old *Pinsel* (paintbrush) factory. Herbert tripped over the word *Pinsel* at least ten times a day. He was both offensive and homesick, forever taunting his new uncle Hugo, who was totally unequipped to deal with a male teenager. Though I did not care much for my belatedly acquired brother, he was much admired by my classmates and thus enhanced my status.

In the spring of 1939, during school recess, I noticed a new girl, who seemed at loose ends. She was short and thin. Her wavy brown hair was carefully cut in a bob. Like me, she was wearing good-quality German children's clothes. Her French was still hesitant. Elizabeth Wolff, like Herbert, had left Germany with a Kindertransport.

Elizabeth came from Berlin. Her parents, both physicians, were almost fifty. It was heartbreaking for them to let their only child go. No friend or family requested Elizabeth, but fate was kind, and Hyman and Mitzie Hollender adopted her temporarily. Both Hyman and Mitzie had come to Belgium from Poland some thirty years earlier. They had three daughters of their own: Ida, Rosie, and Eva. Only Eva, a student at the University of Brussels, still lived at home.

From the day I met Elizabeth, the somewhat dreary recesses became the best part of the schoolday. Elizabeth and I understood each other immediately and instinctively. I finally had a best friend and confidante with whom I could talk about the puzzling and unfair behavior of my parents. Why, I wondered, was my mother so affectionate one day and rejecting the next? Why did my father, to whom I had been so close in Germany, now favor my cute, curly-topped sister?

My German Jewish home, with its familiar food and language, reminded Elizabeth of all she had left behind. At my home Elizabeth, whom my mother nicknamed Sparrow because she was plucky and slight, relaxed the guarded and always cheerful attitude she maintained at the Hollenders. Without seeming ungrateful, she told me how much she missed her parents.

Both Elizabeth and I had a crush on Eva Hollender, a popular, spirited young woman with peroxide-blond hair. Eva taught us about sex and leftist politics. The information she provided about sex, however, was most incomplete, and we avidly read any book we could get hold of. For more information we turned to an antiquated medical encyclopedia that my mother had given to my father "to celebrate the birth of our little Suzanne."

Romantic novels were another important source of information. We particularly liked one called *The Day the Earth Shook*. The title referred to the heroine's loss of virginity. That book too had a handwritten inscription. Dr. Wolff had given it to his bride several months before their marriage. The gift now struck his daughter as very daring. Perhaps grown-ups were less square than we thought.

We had other equally inadequate sources of sex information: movies, my mother's very clumsy explanations, articles in women's magazines, and the whispers of fellow students. Even though sex was of great interest, an active sex life was only a very remote possibility for a fourteen year old like me. At the time all we could possibly hope for was a kiss on the mouth. We sometimes hid behind park benches, spying on lovers, startling them by abruptly emerging from behind a bush as they kissed.

Eva's efforts at political education were more effective. Elizabeth became very skilled at explaining why Communism was the world's only possible salvation. I was not convinced.

The search for an equitable distribution of wealth is as old as mankind itself. Since the Russian Revolution in 1917, the hope of the well-intentioned left fastened on Communism, based on the teachings of Karl Marx and Friedrich Engels. Indeed, the Communist credo stating "to each according to his needs" was extremely appealing. Besides, Communism seemed to be Fascism's only effective answer. Stalin's tactics in Russia, however, indicated that Communism there had resulted in simply another oppressive dictatorship. Nevertheless, liberals espoused the Communist doctrine and some joined the Communist Party, most often clandestinely.

My objections to Communism were more intuitive than rational, and I had little faith in my own convictions. Then, and for years after that, most of the people I respected were Communists, as were the writers whose books sustained my faith in a better world. Could they all be wrong, or was there something wrong with me?

My skepticism seemed to be justified when, in August 1939, the Soviet Union signed a nonaggression pact with Hitler, thereby becoming the führer's ally. Communist all over the world had a tough time explaining Stalin's actions.

On September 1, 1939, the Germans attacked Poland. Britain, who with France had guaranteed Poland's sovereignty, sent an ultimatum, but it did not deter the Germans. By September 3, both Britain and France declared war on Germany. Two weeks later, Russia invaded Poland from the east, demonstrating once more that the USSR was not trustworthy. World War II had started, but for the time being Belgium was at peace.

My grandparents managed to leave Germany for England on September 3. They traveled by sealed train from Frankfurt to Holland, then took a boat from Rotterdam to England. My mother, who loved her father dearly, desperately wanted to see them in Rotterdam, a short train ride from Brussels. The Dutch authorities, however, did not grant her a visa and, after arguing with the consul, she came home crying. "I'll never see my father again," she said. She was right. Opa died in Birmingham in 1941.

The letters Elizabeth received from her parents became increasingly desperate. Reports of German Jews who committed suicide increased; the strength of the Third Reich continued to grow.

Yet while our world fell apart, life's daily routine continued. My father's business, La Synthèse, showed a modest profit. Uncle Fritz and Vati hired a part-time bookkeeper and doubled their workforce from one to two. A hired secretary now helped Tante Hertha with the paperwork.

My mother got better at keeping house, and I improved at doing my chores. Confrontations about washing dishes, fetching coal from the cellar, and shopping diminished. My French was almost flawless, and I finally outgrew my German children's clothes. My mother agreed to let me grow my hair, of which there was so much that it was difficult to tame. I felt that I now looked like everybody else. My parents compromised with Herbert: He went to a boarding school and came home only during holidays.

Chapter 3
May 10, 1940

Children, get up! There is an air raid. We may have to go to the cellar." I stretched in my warm bed and tried to wake. A low, rumbling noise filled the sky.

How silly, I thought. Since when is Mutti afraid of a thunderstorm? Then Vati entered the room. His black, bushy eyebrows were rumpled as usual, but his face was ashen. "The radio reported that the Germans invaded Holland and Belgium at 5:30 A.M.," he said. "We are at war."

I got up, dressed, and went to the kitchen to help make breakfast. Vati, a coffee addict, had taught me how to make his favorite brew when I was eight years old. Mutti soft-boiled the eggs. The fresh rolls were delivered to our front door as if nothing unusual was afoot. We ate a lot more than on ordinary mornings—my family always eats when upset. The radio said that there was no school.

I made my bed in the traditional German manner. This meant stripping the two sheets and the blanket, puffing up the pillow, and airing everything for at least thirty minutes near an open window. Then the bed was reassembled. That morning I skipped the airing. The day already dragged, though it was only eight o'clock.

According to the radio, the situation was confusing, but clearly Hitler's blitzkrieg—a war in which the army advances at the speed of lightning—

seemed, once more, to be a success. By approaching France through Holland and Belgium, his troops avoided the Maginot Line, France's allegedly impenetrable fortification. Both the Belgian and Dutch armies reeled under the impact of the German onslaught. Britain and France sent troops. Would they arrive in time to halt the German advance? (See appendix, map 1.)

Airplanes kept passing overhead and sirens blared constantly. There were no bombs. After a while, the antiaircraft guns responded with a feeble *tac-tac-tac.* One got quickly used to the constant racket.

My parents closed their bedroom door and debated our plan of action. They decided that we would leave Brussels at once. Vati went to the factory to fetch the car.

Soon after he left, the doorbell rang. Two officers of the Belgian Secret Service had come to arrest us because we were foreign nationals. Being German, we were deemed particularly dangerous! My mother, Gaby, and I followed the officers downstairs and boarded an elegant hearse pressed into service to round up other folks like us. The hearse already held a half-dozen foreigners, most of them refugees. My mother said that real traitors would not have been dumb enough to stay at home or answer the doorbell. After collecting a few more "undesirables," the hearse delivered us to my school, which now served as a makeshift detention center.

Three hundred people filled the auditorium. All were stunned by the war, which we had feared and fantasized about and which had finally engulfed us. My sister and I sat next to my mother. I fidgeted—I was never good at sitting still. I looked for a familiar face, but there was none. How I wished Elizabeth was there. I knew that she was safe, because the Hollenders were Belgian citizens. There were other children. Right across from us sat a girl with brown curly hair and a long face. She had pencil and paper and played a game with her father.

More people arrived, including Vati. The secret police had picked him up when he returned to our apartment after getting the car. My friend Suzy arrived with her parents and her three desirable brothers whom until then I had admired only from afar. The boys organized a ball game for everybody. The girl with the long face joined. Her name was Dédé Hirschland. We horsed around in the schoolyard. At noon there was soup. I volunteered to dish it out and cheered up.

Then I saw Madame Tordeur, the school principal. As usual, she petrified me, but when she saw me she came over and sadly shook my hand. All of a sudden I understood the seriousness of our situation. I left my new friends and sat next to my mother.

My parents berated themselves for not having taken our valuables, warm clothes, or blankets when suddenly arrested. Since this was my school, we knew the custodian. My mother asked whether he would let me slip out a back door to go home to fetch some essentials. He agreed, but insisted that his fifteen-year-old son, Paul, escort me. Paul and I walked to our apartment along the streets I knew so well from passing through them four times a day. "Vive Napoleon" and "A bas Napoleon" was still scrawled on one of the walls we passed, a reminder of the fierce partisanship that had accompanied Mademoiselle Feytmans's history class a few weeks earlier.

My mother gave me strict instructions on what to do when I got home: Pack the platinum laboratory ware, the passports, the address book, the hidden cash, and sweaters and blankets. Her most urgent request, however, concerned an old revolver she kept in the nightstand. She had bought the weapon years ago when we had rented a lonely beach house in Arenshop, a resort on the Baltic Sea. I never understood why she hung on to the gun. Now my mother felt that it was highly incriminating and told me to hide it. To do that, I had to distract Paul. Fortunately, he took the air raids more seriously than I did, and I convinced him to wait for me in the cellar. It was there that I hid the gun in a pile of coal.

By chance we had a lot of cash. Two days earlier my father had cashed a large check, which actually belonged to a friend waiting for his American visa in Britain. The friend knew that if he were to cash the check in London, his assets would be frozen. So he had asked my father to transfer the money directly to the United States. My father had not been able to deposit the money that day, and we had about $10,000 in our possession. This was a large sum in 1940 and increased our financial security in the years to come.

Exciting as it was, my expedition turned out to have been pointless. Soon after I returned to school, the women, children, and non-enemy aliens were released. My mother, Gaby, and I once more retraced the familiar steps home.

Some of the men were freed for a variety of reasons: among them, health, an important job, or a letter of recommendation. My father was detained. The next morning my sister and I took him some additional clothes and personal belongings. He met us at the entrance to the school. He wore his hat, tilted at the familiar cocky angle, a pipe clenched between his crooked front teeth, and smiled. We promised to come back the next day and casually kissed him good-bye. That evening, however, the men were transferred to a more central detention center and from there they left by train. Nobody knew to where, but all suspected that it was France. My mother was now in sole charge. Like most of our friends and many ordinary civilians, we decided to go south to France. Because my mother was a bad driver, we returned the car to the factory and went to the railroad station in search of a train.

The direct rail lines to Paris, a mere 150 miles away, were reserved for the military. Civilians had to travel by a circuitous route. We decided to reach France via Flanders and the coastal road. This meant taking the train to Ostend, then boarding a trolley that ran along the entire Belgian coastline. We planned to cross the French border at Bray Dunes, near the popular seaside resort of La Panne.

It seemed sensible to go to the Belgian coast. During World War I, German troops never occupied Belgium's most western corner. There the then-mighty German army simply could not cross the rather insignificant Yser River. From 1914 to 1918, La Panne was the headquarters of the Belgian army and the home of King Albert—the soldier-king; Elizabeth, his queen; and their three children, including Leopold—the present king. It was still a matter of pride that during World War I the Belgian army never entirely left its own soil.

There was complete pandemonium at the railroad station. Civilians fleeing from the Germans tried to get into the station. French and British soldiers, dispatched to reinforce the Belgian troops, tried to get out. The sight of the friendly soldiers reassured us. They were young and confident, and they sang. Their repertoire included new war songs like "We Shall Hang Out Our Laundry on the Siegfried Line"—the German defense complex—and familiar oldies from World War I, such as "My Bonnie Lies Over the Ocean" and "It's a Long Way to Tipperary." I hoped that these soldiers would be able to protect us.

Belgium is a tiny country. Even in 1940, trains that cover the seventy-odd miles between Brussels and coastal Ostend normally took only two to three hours. We knew this because, together with other beach-bound passengers, we had traveled this very same route the summer before. How different it was today. The people looked grim and they carried an assortment of bags and bundles.

We waited in the station. From time to time, a train was announced. Everybody pushed, but often there was no train. Finally, there was one and we managed to get aboard. We even got seats. The train was so full, however, that one could hardly breathe. When it finally pulled out of the station, it proceeded at an agonizing pace, stopping often. Troop trains had the right of way. For hours we sat outside the town of Ghent. Planes flew overhead and the air-raid sirens blared, but there were no bombs. Later it transpired that the station master in Ghent was a traitor who provided the Germans with detailed information about railroad traffic.

Twenty-four hours later we arrived in Ostend. It was May 14, my fifteenth birthday. We were tired and needed a bed, but no hotel or rooming house would give us a room when they heard my mother's strong German accent. Eventually, a woman took pity because she assumed that, like herself, my mother was a widow burdened by young children.

As soon as we fell into bed, the air-raid siren sounded again. This time there were bombs. The hotel was completely dark as nobody yet had blackout curtains. My mother lit our way to the basement by flashlight. "You, *sale Boche*"—a curse word often used to describe the Germans—a fellow guest screamed. "You traitor! Are you signaling to the planes?" My mother hastily turned off her light, but our spirits sank.

The next day we set out for the French border. By then we knew that we had taken too many suitcases. We left most of them at the hotel in Ostend. We still kept too many bags. Each of us lugged a heavy one. My mother also carried an immense leather handbag, which at night she strapped to her waist. Gaby and I christened the bag Fredericke, claiming that it was our mother's favorite "child." Fredericke held our money, papers, and other treasures. We did not know until much later that some potassium cyanide poison was hidden inside Fredericke's lining so that, if necessary, my mother could end our lives.

By now thousands of refugees filled Ostend and the entire Belgian coast. I knew that the Jews had good reason to get away, but why did the rest of the Belgian population flee from the Germans? From Ostend we took a streetcar to La Panne, a distance of some 18 miles. From there we walked to Bray Dunes, the border post.

Ordinary passenger cars lined the road from La Panne to Bray Dunes. The vehicles were overloaded with people and belongings. Strapped to the roofs were chairs, suitcases, bicycles, and mattresses, which now warded off stray bullets. Most of the passengers stood next to their cars, hoping that France, the promised land, would open its borders. The scene was a modern version of the Jewish exodus from Egypt. Progress on foot was faster than by car.

As we walked along the highway, I spotted Elizabeth standing next to the Hollender's overloaded car. After we got over the joy of this unexpected meeting, we embraced sadly, not knowing whether we would ever meet again.

It always surprises me how quickly human enterprise responds to a perceived need. As soon as the roads filled with throngs of civilians, staggering under their unwieldy belongings, there were men who, for a modest fee, willingly transported their luggage in wheelbarrows. We now were in the Flemish-speaking part of Belgium, and the operators of this makeshift transport system spoke Flemish rather than French.

We promptly hired a pushcart and were temporarily relieved of our burdens. Since the cart was not quite full, my mother allowed a lonely refugee woman to add her suitcase to ours. As we plodded on, our new companion excitedly jabbered away in German. Hearing the hated tongue, our driver dumped our suitcases into the ditch, calling us "damned *Boche.*" My mother, mastering her entire Flemish vocabulary, said: *"Niks Boche."* The man finally relented, reloaded, and rolled us as close to the border as he could.

In times of crises, it is very important to have the necessary identification papers or documents. Identification papers were all important during World War II, and in time I became an expert.

In Belgium the town hall of each borough issues photo-identification cards to all persons over the age of fifteen. The identity cards are necessary for many transactions, such as collecting registered letters at the post office, providing proof of age, or using a public library. Identity cards list date of birth, home address, and nationality. At the time, Belgian citizens had green cards; foreigners with a long-term residence status had yellow cards. Those of us who had to renew our residence status every few months had white cards, crossed with a large red stripe.

We were definitely pariahs. We were Jews, enemy aliens, and had a very short residence permit. Our identity cards were white with a red stripe. In other words, they were highly undesirable.

To make matters more complicated, Germany had expatriated some of its former Jewish citizens, declaring them to be stateless, while others remained German nationals. The decision as to who was stateless and who remained a German national was totally arbitrary. We were German nationals and thus enemy aliens. The French allowed Belgians and citizens from friendly countries to cross the border into France.

So many people wanted to cross the French border that the guards did not have time to scrutinize the documents of each individual. Instead the guards asked groups of about ten persons to hold up their identification. If the cards were all green, they let the group pass. Because of the difference in color and the red stripe, the border guard usually, but not always, spotted the identity cards of foreigners. Some foreigners were lucky and were allowed to enter France. We did not make it. "We'll try tomorrow," my mother said. We engaged another pushcart, returned to La Panne, and found a room.

The next day we returned to the border, tried to pass, and failed again. This time, however, we decided to sit it out at the border. We joined the makeshift camp of other "refuseniks" that had sprung up among the sand dunes. Luck would have it that we settled close to the Hirschlands, whose daughter Dédé I had met while imprisoned in my school.

Her mother, Alma, recognized us and came over to introduce herself to my mother. Almost immediately, she asked about our nationality. My mother said that we were German. Mrs. Hirschland cheered a bit. "We have a problem," she said. "My aunt Lene lives with us while waiting for her U.S. visa. She is a German national; we are stateless. There is a rumor that tomorrow the French will admit the stateless. I don't know what to do. Could you possibly take on Tante Lene?" We needed a sixty-five-year-old woman like a hole in the head, but my mother agreed to look after her.

We moved our camp closer to that of the Hirschlands and continued to wait. I was grateful to have company. I talked to Dédé and could not take my eyes off Gert, the older of her two brothers. He was tall, had curly brown hair, and always chewed on a blade of grass. Pitt, Dédé's other brother, had moody eyes and full lips; his curly hair was darker. Pitt kept his distance.

The next morning we again gathered our belongings and assaulted the border post repeatedly. The guards, however, always spotted our despicable identity card. During one of these sorties, a man tapped my mother's shoulder. It was Harry Salomon.

Harry was my uncle Otto's best friend. During World War I, the two men fought together in the German army. Their battalion spent almost four years in the trenches near the Belgian coast. After the war Harry fell in love with my mother and had wanted to marry her, but she had declined.

In Germany Harry ran the wine business founded by his grandfather Marx. The firm had well-to-do customers in Brussels. When Hitler came to power, Harry and his wife, Gretel, and their son, Martin, had emigrated to Belgium.

We had visited the Salomons when we arrived in Brussels in 1938, and Harry's old love for my mother was rekindled. His joy of running into us here at the French border was great. Since he and his family also did not manage to cross into France, the Salomons moved their camp next to ours and that of the Hirschlands. Seventeen-year-old Martin enlarged the teenage contingent.

My mother and I heaved a sigh of relief to have found company. Perhaps the men would know what to do. There were daily strategy meetings on how to get past the border guards. One day Pitt Hirschland managed to get across, carrying with him his mother's suitcase and burdening her with a constant concern for his well-being.

Once there was a rumor that a train was leaving for Paris. We rushed to the station already mobbed by other hopefuls. "Children," my mother said, "tomorrow we'll be in Paris. How I wish that I had taken decent clothes with me. My raw silk suit, which just came back from the cleaner, would be perfect." There was no train, and, after a long wait, we returned to our camp in the dunes.

It gradually became pointless to try to cross the border. Some people claimed that the Germans had circumvented the armies massed in Belgium and that it was now impossible for us to reach the heart of France.

Indeed, by May 22, an increasing number of refugees returned from France, telling everybody of the bad treatment they had received. Some told us that the French even refused to give them water, advising them mockingly to "drink the water of your Albert Canal," the pride of the Belgian defense system. The canal had been designed to safeguard the Belgian heartland, but, like all the other fortifications designed for a more old-fashioned war, it had crumbled under Hitler's onslaught.

On May 30, the Bamberger-Hirschland-Salomon contingent decided to "abandon" the border and returned to La Panne. We hoped we would be safe there. "The Germans will never get here," proclaimed Mr. Salomon. "To conquer La Panne, they must cross the Yser River. When I was in the German army during World War I, we tried crossing that river for four long years."

Harry Salomon and the rest of the world were learning that an abyss separated the tactics of World War I and World War II. There were no newspapers, and it was difficult even to listen to the radio. Besides, the news was unreliable. The British maintained a news blackout; the German propaganda machine gloated about the success of the blitzkrieg. We did not know what to believe.

Later we learned that on May 20, a few days after we left Brussels, the Germans indeed had reached the French coast at Abbeville, less than 100 miles southwest of La Panne. This maneuver cut off the British Expeditionary Force (BEF) from the rest of France. As the German troops advanced toward the English Channel, the pocket that held the BEF became smaller and smaller. By the middle of May the English were already considering withdrawing some of their troops from Continental Europe. A week later, the entire British Expeditionary Force (BEF) was threatened with annihilation.

The German troops were pressing hard toward the three Channel ports—Calais, Boulogne, and Dunkirk—from which the soldiers could be rescued. By May 27 the Allies had to abandon Calais and Boulogne. This left only Dunkirk, some ten miles from our camp at the Belgian border and fifteen miles from La Panne. British, French, and Belgian troops were bravely holding on to the small pocket of land that included their escape corridor.

Small decisions often determine the fate of a battle. On May 24, as the German panzers (tanks) were about to conquer the pocket that held Dunkirk and La Panne, Hitler halted his troops for three days. The resulting lull did not change the plight of the trapped troops or the refugees fleeing the Germans. It did, however, allow Britain to rethink its rescue efforts. In spite of the news blackout, the British population guessed that disaster was about to strike their BEF. Within days all those who owned any kind of seagoing vessel moored along the Thames and the Channel coast volunteered their boats and services. A huge armada of fishing trawlers, tugs, motor launches, excursion boats, freighters, cabin cruisers, dredges, and ferries joined in the rescue operation.

Leopold III capitulated on May 28. The Belgian troops defending the flank of the escape corridor hoisted a white flag. The British and French closed the gap as best they could, covering the retreat of the Allied troops to the beach between La Panne and Dunkirk. The orders given to the British troops were to gather on the beaches and await transport home.

Half a million soldiers poured onto the beaches. Bigger boats started lifting soldiers from the Belgian and French coasts by May 24. They had limited capacity, and, given the strength of the Germans, it was estimated that only one-tenth of the BEF would be rescued. The disarray among the British and French soldiers was complete.

Then the tide turned. By May 27, when the Germans resumed their active warfare, their air force—the Luftwaffe—was grounded by the mist that shrouded the beaches, and the usually rough North Sea was calm. A semblance of order returned among the Allied troops. Embarkation jetties were built from now-useless trucks. On May 30, the astonished soldiers witnessed the arrival of the "little ships" that would bring them home to safety.

Ignoring details of the battle that engulfed us, we returned to La Panne as a group. Harry Salomon and Pappy Hirschland assumed the high command of our little contingent and weighed the next move. I walked next to Gert or Dédé; Gaby clung to my mother. Gretel Salomon and Alma Hirschland took turns encouraging Tante Lene to put one foot in front of the other.

We planned to stay in "safe" La Panne and looked for a house. This was easy. In peacetime, La Panne was a thriving summer colony, with many seasonal rentals. We quickly found a villa whose caretaker accepted a deposit of two weeks' rent.

The name of our shingled villa was *Lust en Rust* (Joy and Rest). It had cozy casement windows, many bedrooms, wicker furniture, a big kitchen, and a charming garden. An imposing crystal chandelier hung in the dining room. The owners must have cherished it, since a sign on the wall cautioned renters not to touch the lamp. There was a croquet set in the storage room, which Gert and I set up immediately.

The women started cleaning the house, washing sheets, and airing the rooms. The rest of us tried to buy as much food as we could. The shelves of the grocery stores had been stripped by the hordes of refugees who had descended onto this normally quiet resort. Staple foods were gone, but luxury items such as pickled olives, salted nuts, canned pâté, and marinated artichoke hearts were still available.

The bakery baked once a day and rationed the loaves, one per person. I lined up in front of the shop long before the bread came out of the oven. After a ninety-minute wait, I proudly secured my loaf. To get to and from the bakery, I had to cross the large, open town square. The German planes that patrolled the sky were harassed by antiaircraft guns. The noise of the guns and an occasional stray bullet echoed back and forth among the houses lining the square. It was as if bullets exploded all around me. My knees felt weak, and I was so scared that I felt like lying down.

I did get back to *Lust en Rust*. Gretel Salomon had concocted a hot stew that we ate hungrily. It was the first warm meal we had had in some time. For no good reason our spirits were high.

The bed linen was not quite dry, but my impatient mother nevertheless used it to make our beds. Harry Salomon joined her in our bedroom and, not seeing me, gave her a kiss on the mouth. I was shocked.

We were bone-tired and glad to undress and wash off the sand and dirt we had collected in the dunes. Then we gratefully fell into bed—but not for very long.

At one o'clock in the morning, the shelling began. My mother shook me awake and dragged me down to the small coal cellar. I sat on top of a pile of coals and tried to stay awake, but I kept dozing off. The sound of the guns followed a curious pattern—it came very loudly from one side of the house and very weakly from the other. The strong explosions shook the house. Whenever I got too anxious, I looked at Gert, whose face never lost its calm. Harry sweated profusely and mopped his pate with a dirty handkerchief. Pappy held Alma; Gaby hid her head in my mother's lap.

All of a sudden the dark cellar filled with a dancing orange light. Pappy ventured outside. The house next door had caught fire, which might spread to ours, he told us. Still it was safer for us to stay put in the cellar.

After one of my little naps, I discovered that a soldier wearing a Belgian uniform had joined us. "The king has surrendered, and the British are leaving," he said. "The weak cannon fire you hear is from the guns of the ships covering their retreat; the strong explosions are from German artillery fire." Then the soldier started cursing the British, Belgians, French, Germans, and Jews.

By morning the shooting finally stopped, and we ventured upstairs. *Lust en Rust* was in shambles. The explosions had shattered many windowpanes, shredding the curtains. Glass splinters floated in the leftover meat stew. A piece of shrapnel lay on my pillow. Destruction had spared the chandelier in the dining room, however, and it was now the only totally unscathed furnishing in the house.

Our "high command" met and decided to return to Brussels at once. Wearily, we repacked the suitcases, ate some of the bread I had conquered the day before, and started our trek home. Furnes, the next bigger town, was our first goal.

Poor Tante Lene was so exhausted that she could barely walk. It took all of Alma's strength to convince her to carry on. On the outskirts of La Panne, we met a man with the now-familiar wheelbarrow and asked him to ferry our luggage to Furnes. He refused, saying that he would not return to Furnes for all the money in the world. Soon we knew why.

Stray bullets and shrapnel had killed most of the abandoned cattle. Their carcasses now littered the pastures, their stiff legs pointing beseechingly skyward. Swarms of flies feasted on their remains.

The villages that stretch almost continuously along Belgium's rural roads were deserted. Once we came upon a motionless, huddled man. "Did you see that corpse?" I asked Gert, trying to sound cool and brave. I was, however, sick to my stomach and listened to Pappy, who told me and Dédé to look as straight in front of us as we possibly could.

Refugees like us, who had not managed to flee the Nazis, filled the roads. German planes flew even lower than before, but the antiaircraft guns were silent.

The weather contrasted with the sorry state of the world. The sky was blue, the sun shining. Spring flowers were out, and the lilacs, roses, and apple trees bloomed. The birds sang. My heart too brimmed over with spring. Gert was the most wonderful person I had ever met. I loved his rough skin, his calm, his sense of humor. And he was all mine. As we trudged endlessly along the roads of Flanders, he was glad of my company and enjoyed my stories. The present took over; I even forgot Elizabeth.

We shuffled along for about two or three hours, then Harry and Pappy decided that we had to find quarters for the night. We found a suitable farm, and the owner agreed to let us use the hayloft. Pappy managed to buy a dozen raw eggs. Dédé and I first refused to suck the glob from the cracked eggshell, but eventually we did.

After I bedded down in the hay I thought about the war, my father, and Gert, and I prayed to God as I had when I was a child. I soon fell asleep.

The next morning we breakfasted on dry toast and more raw eggs and set out again. We bought a baby carriage from our host, the farmer, and loaded it with some of our luggage.

Gert pushed the baby carriage and I, in seventh heaven, tried to amuse him. I sang some of the Girl Scout songs I had learned in what now seemed a previous life. Though I sing like a crow, Gert claimed that he enjoyed listening.

By three o'clock Harry again started to worry about quarters for the night. My mother wanted to hurry home and had a fit, but Mr. Salomon prevailed and we found another hayloft. To reach it we had to climb a steep ladder.

When Tante Lene saw the ladder and the steer housed beneath it, she revolted and refused to join the rest of us. Alma, Tante Lene in tow, went to see the owner of the barn. Because the older woman did not speak a single word of French, Alma told her aunt to keep silent. Wanting to hide our being German, Alma explained that her aunt was an American. "She is too old to climb the ladder," Alma said. "Can she stay in the house?" The farmer agreed, expressing his delight at having an American guest.

"Let me fetch my neighbor," he said. "He used to live in America and loves to speak English." Tante Lene's English was as nonexistent as her French, but finally Alma managed to put her tired and disoriented aunt to bed.

It was too early to go to sleep. Gert, Martin, Dédé, Gaby, and I sat around and told each other ghost stories. I was happy and felt guilty about feeling content.

Additional refugees piled into the hayloft, among them a group of Orthodox Jews. In the morning, when I went to the outhouse, I noticed each of them fastening a black box to his forehead and winding leather thongs around his arm and hand. Then they swayed, prayed, and bowed to the East. I had never seen anyone worship in this traditional manner.

The next day as we continued our journey, we ran into German soldiers. I trembled, but need not have worried. The soldiers were young, blond, and good-looking. As some of the fellow refugees remarked, "They were so very sweet and polite, not at all as they had been during World War I." The Germans distributed chocolate, cigarettes, and, most important, transportation back home to Brussels. The soldiers had orders to be as pleasant as possible; besides, the refugee-clogged roads hampered troop movement.

We were too scared to accept the ride offered by the Germans. Being stateless, Harry and Pappy were worried about being executed on the spot, but the Germans had other priorities.

We booked passage on a truck operated by an enterprising Belgian civilian and returned to Brussels on June 4, exactly three weeks after we had left. On that same day, the last of the British Expeditionary Force left from Dunkirk. Miraculously, 338,000 of the 400,000 troops trapped on the beaches near La Panne were rescued. These men would be the nucleus of an army that might one day come back and liberate us.

In Brussels our apartment welcomed us. The modern bathroom, my bed, the kitchen, and the heavy German furniture looked most inviting. My mother's freshly cleaned raw silk suit lay on the couch. School was open and I went the very next day. The Hollenders too returned, and I told Elizabeth all about Gert. We had both grown up during the past weeks. Elizabeth's concern about her parents was even greater than before, and I too now was fatherless.

Chapter 4

The Same but Different

The warmth with which my fellow students greeted me upon my return touched me deeply. The class was smaller. None of the other Jewish children had returned, and nobody knew their whereabouts. Among the absentees were two of my special tormentors: Nina de Tchernic and Ida Kaminsky.

A few of the teachers were also missing. Some were on probation; they had fled the Germans in spite of an order issued by the Ministry of Education to be available in case schoolchildren needed to be evacuated. Others, like my French teacher, Madame Massard, left with permission because her husband, a government employee, was ordered to escape to England. The Massards did not reach Great Britain but the prime minister and other members of the Belgian government did. They established a government-in-exile in London, which provided moral support to occupied Belgium and hung on to Belgium's colony. The immense mineral resources of the Belgian Congo—now Zaire—supplied the Allies with uranium and other essential raw materials.

Deciding to share the fate of the Belgian soldiers imprisoned in Germany, King Leopold III opted for house arrest in his castle in Brussels. His decision, many people felt, was based on the unpopular but perhaps realistic expectation that Germany might win the war. By staying in Belgium, the king safeguarded his throne. Leopold's popularity plunged further when he wedded the daughter of a Flemish politician and possible black-market profiteer. This marriage not only ridiculed the king's intention to live like his imprisoned soldiers, but offended the many who cherished the memory of his first wife, the universally beloved Queen Astrid.

The Rexists—the Belgian Fascists—and their leader Leon Degrelle were in their glory. They strutted about in uniform and greeted others with a loud "Heil Hitler!" The Germans appointed as many collaborators as they could to key government positions.

At the lycée our rigid education marched on in spite of the cataclysm that engulfed the world. Substitutes took the place of the absent teachers. We continued to dissect complex French sentences and analyze each line of plays by Corneille, Racine, and Molière. The class rose to my defense when a substitute took me to task because of the many spelling errors that, as usual, riddled my weekly essays. I was relieved when Madame Massard returned.

Mademoiselle Feytmans's history classes continued to be pure delight. That year we were studying the history of Western Europe. The recent events permitted her to compare the campaigns of the Third Reich with those of Napoleon. By then I knew already that it was much better to study history in retrospect than to live through it.

In spite of the superficial normalcy, life was schizophrenic. We did not know what had happened to my father except that he was one of thousands of political prisoners—a mixture of foreign nationals and a few Rexists—who had been transferred by train to France. Rumor had it that the train, endlessly shunted around France, had been bombed and that the French guards maltreated some of the internees. Within days of our return, my mother hurried to the office of the Red Cross. There indeed had been a few casualties, one even was called Bamberger, but it was not my father. The internees were now in camps in the south of France.

Nobody trusted the news issued by the Germans, so listening to the British Broadcasting Corporation (BBC) became a nightly ritual. The British radio, however, was also not very encouraging. Strengthening his bonds with the winning team, Mussolini had declared war on Britain and France on June 10, 1940. Paris had fallen on June 14, and France surrendered on the twenty-second. With a macabre sense of history, Hitler insisted that the armistice be signed in the same railroad car in the forest of Compiégne, in which the Allies had accepted the German surrender at the end of World War I.

Since the United States remained neutral, Britain and its brave and eloquent prime minister, Winston Churchill, were the only friends we had left. For what seemed an eternity, they remained our only feeble hope.

It was of course strictly illegal to listen to the BBC. The Germans, however, had a tough time making the Belgians obey any of their orders. The memory of the World War I German occupation, which had ended only a short twenty-two years earlier, was still fresh. The majority of the population hated the Nazis with a vengeance.

Open resistance was impossible, but the Germans were harassed in many small ways. Burning their uniforms with cigarettes on crowded streetcars was a favorite sport. The Germans tried to retaliate, but the hostility of the population was so pervasive that punitive measures simply aggravated the situation.

Whenever I found it useful, I spoke broken German with a heavy French accent. Once, when a platoon of German soldiers asked me for directions, I responded in pidgin German, sending the group the wrong way. Then I waited. After ten minutes the platoon returned. Another soldier again suggested asking "the little black-haired miss" for directions. His commander told him that they had already done so, but I did not know the way. I returned home giggling.

Actually, during the initial three months of the occupation, the Germans were extremely conciliatory. The sixty-one-year-old Prussian general who headed the current administration, Alexander von Falkenhausen, made a concerted effort to avoid some of the mistakes made during the World War I occupation.

Von Falkenhausen was an old-fashioned army man, more interested in winning the war than rounding up Jews. He also feared that open persecution of the Jews would ruffle Belgian feathers. He informed Berlin that there were few Jews in Belgium—70,000 all told—and that these were no threat. Higher German authorities humored him temporarily. Von

Falkenhausen assured the Belgian authorities that Jews would not be persecuted, and it was tempting to believe that matters would remain calm.

At first the events favored von Falkenhausen's attitude. Western Europe's rapid collapse, and the near certitude that Hitler would win the war, had engendered such a state of shock that some of Belgium's industrial leaders were willing to compromise. They would produce goods for the German war effort, but no Belgian workers would be forcibly deported to Germany, as they had been during the First World War. The Germans also instituted a voluntary labor recruitment program, which initially was very successful.

By October 1940 the honeymoon had come to an end. The Germans had systematically plundered Belgium of its raw materials. Food and fuel became scarce. Food supplies were rationed, and food stamps were distributed monthly at the town hall of each borough. The food rations were way below subsistence. During the winter of 1940–41, most everybody was hungry and, since coal was also in short supply, cold. The black market, which would eventually supplement the totally inadequate rations, was still in its infancy.

The Germans' indifference to the Jews also did not last. In October 1940 they ordered the Belgian authorities to register the Jews. Clerks at the town hall stamped our identification cards with a big *J*. All in all 56,000 Jews were registered. Hindsight is easy: Many of the Jews who did not register escaped persecution and annihilation. As in Germany, Jewish stores, restaurants, and hotels had to identify themselves as such, and Jews could no longer be teachers, lawyers, or journalists.

For the time being, these restrictions had few practical consequences, but our fear and uncertainty increased. What were the Germans going to do to the Jews? We knew that in 1939 the Nazis started to "resettle" to Poland any Polish Jews living in Germany. Though there were no details, we knew that Eastern Europe was hell. Could we still go to America if and when our visas came through? What were we going to do for money?

Von Falkenhausen did not manage to protect the Jews, but his rather benign attitude had a profound impact on our fate. Jews in Belgium fared much better than those in neighboring Holland, which was governed by a civilian administration headed by the Gestapo and Artur Seyss-Inquart, a renowned Jew-hater.

♦

As soon as we returned to Brussels, my mother visited La Synthèse, my father's small chemical factory. Uncle Fritz had also been deported as a German enemy alien. Poor, childless Tante Hertha felt so abandoned and despondent that she had poisoned her beloved dachshund. Like two million other citizens, she tried to escape to France; she failed, returned to Brussels, and committed suicide. My mother felt guilty. "Why did I not ask her to come with us when we left Brussels?" she kept repeating. I missed Tante Hertha. Her death, so reminiscent of that of my aunt Paula, filled me with dread and foreboding.

When my mother showed up at La Synthèse, the entire staff—three people in all—greeted her with dismay. They had assumed that we would not return and counted on inheriting the business. The accountant and one of the factory hands had already contacted some of my father's customers My mother fired the staff and for a while kept the business going. She successfully sold the small stock of food colors and nitrates to the food industry, and even managed to conclude a few transactions on her own. She also started to liquidate the equipment. It was the first and last time in her life that my mother worked outside her house—and she liked it. Although she had no accountant, the extremely attentive Harry Salomon, whose own wine business had come to an abrupt halt, was happy to help her.

In the evening after my mother came home from work and increased her consumption of tincture of valerian, a folk remedy alleged to have tranquilizing properties, she yelled even more than usual about my slovenly habits. She also cried a lot. I attributed all that to the strain of the war. One evening, after Gaby had gone to bed, she told me that the disgruntled accountant had mailed her a packet of passionate love letters addressed to my father. I now knew the reason for her grief. The letters were from Maria Botmann, my father's former German secretary. The discovery hurt, especially because we all were extremely fond of Miss Botmann and considered her a good friend.

In Hanover one of my favorite treats had been to spend a day with my father at his chemical plant. The factory was in Lehrte, a small town, thirty minutes by train from Hanover. There, in addition to manufacturing fine chemicals, my father engaged in his hobby: gardening. Over the years he had created a big garden with lawns, flower beds, vegetable patches, berry bushes, and dozens of fruit trees. In the middle of it all stood a little pink garden house. Even now, I imagine that the Garden of Eden is just like my father's.

I roamed that garden. When it rained I sheltered in the garden house. When the sun was out, I climbed the willow tree and sat there for hours reading and rereading favorite books: *Winnie the Pooh, Mary Poppins, Tom Sawyer,* the Greek hero tales . . . I also tended the little plot my father had assigned me. I specialized in radishes and lettuce, because they grew so fast. Mostly, however, I daydreamed and stuffed myself with raspberries, cherries, strawberries, peaches, apples, and pears until my stomach could hold no more. I was particularly fond of a tree that bore yellow cherries. One day my father gave it to me.

The gift was only symbolic, since all the fruit was ours. Canning it was a big chore loyally performed by Anna. Symbol or not, I was happy to own the cherry tree.

I avoided intruding on my father's workday and saw him only during lunch, a time we both treasured. But I was far from lonely. My father's longtime and devoted staff knew me since birth and enjoyed fussing over me. I visited the laboratories, offices, and even the factory itself. Everybody had a treat. The chemists let me turn water into "blood." The secretaries let me type. The factory hands showed me how the chemicals crystallized out of their mother liquor.

During the day some employees came to spend time with me in the garden, Miss Botmann among them. Once she came as my yellow cherries were ripe, and I kept popping them into my mouth. "Your father gave me that tree," she said. "I don't mind if you have some cherries." I could hardly believe my ears.

I confronted my father and reminded him that he had given away *my* tree. He did not offer to rectify his error, but simply shrugged his shoulders and told me to pick another tree. I was puzzled and sad, but did not know why.

Miss Botmann had continued to do us various favors. When we left Germany, Gaby and I had to give her Peter, our beloved, faithful fox terrier, whom we could not take with us. I could not believe that for years Miss Botmann had been my father's mistress. I remembered the cherry tree and was furious. I again wanted to confront my father, but he was not there!

I knew that the affair was much more serious for my mother than for me. Moreover, she was entirely responsible for our safety. My job was to sustain her as best I could, though I often felt at odds with her unreasonable demands about my behavior. I stifled my resentment and shelved my own fears. I realized that my mother had to cope with decisions that would determine whether we would live or die.

By July we finally heard from my father directly. He indeed was interned in Saint Cyprien, a camp in unoccupied France. The French had built this and other camps for refugees who had escaped the Spanish Civil War.

My father's letters described the misery of these camps. Food was poor and insufficient; the French guards were callous. When it rained the camp turned into a mud flat, and the roofs of the barracks leaked. The nights were bitter cold and he froze. There was dysentery. My father and some of his friends managed to prepare charcoal, an old remedy for diarrhea, by incomplete combustion of animal bones.

His greatest disappointment, however, was the selfishness, dishonesty, and lack of civility of his fellow inmates. There was no true companionship; stealing and squealing were commonplace.

We sent my father packages and wrote letters. I knew that I should be sadder and more concerned than I was. I could not, because I resented Miss Botmann and the fact that he had cheated on us all for so many years.

My cousin Herbert Sterner was also in Saint Cyprien. He remained hostile and rejecting. My father reported that Herbert ignored him completely and never even asked about the fate of his aunt and cousins. "Stupid boy," my father wrote. "I would help him, give him some food."

Many other internees had been separated from their wives and children. One of these families was our neighbors in Brussels. We contacted the Beissingers and became friends.

When France surrendered and signed an armistice with Germany, the Nazis occupied most of the country. The south of France remained "free," its capital being the town of Vichy. The titular head of this so-called unoccupied France, or "free zone," was Marshal Henri Philippe Pétain, a World War I hero. He was surrounded by Fascist ministers. The Vichy government openly joined the German war effort, and many French Jews were deported. During 1940 and most of 1941, however, one could still escape from Europe legally, and unoccupied France was the major point of departure.

Unoccupied France was already loaded with refugees who had successfully gotten there during the German spring offensive. Now all these people tried to obtain visas to leave Europe. Visas to the United States were the most prized.

Before anyone got an actual visa, he or she was interrogated lengthily by the employees of the consulate, although such hearings did not guarantee a visa. Before and during World War II, consuls and their delegates had unlimited power over people's lives. Many functionaries enjoyed playing cat and mouse. They were extremely fickle as to who would get a visa and who would not. Sometimes they decided on their own; sometimes they had received orders from home; sometimes they could be bribed.

Information about the exact behavior, likes, and policies of the consular personnel was most useful. For instance, a few people knew that the United States was almost halting the issuance of visas before President Roosevelt's reelection in November 1940. Postponing an unfavorable hearing date until after the election often made the difference between life and death. Small South American countries also issued visas—some genuine, some false.

Refugees who miraculously obtained the proper papers could leave southern France legally via Spain and Portugal. From there boats took them to freedom.

Not everybody waited for the appropriate legal papers. Spain was Hitler's ally, and Switzerland had long ago sealed its borders to refugees. Nevertheless, throughout the war, refugees attempted to flee France by "crawling" across the Pyrenees into Spain or the Alps into Switzerland. Some refugees were accepted, but many were refused admission, sent back, and then picked up by German or French border guards.

Since my father's camp was in unoccupied France, my mother and her new friend, Mrs. Beissinger, debated endlessly about whether we should try to join the men. My mother was against it, but Mrs. Beissinger decided to go.

To reach unoccupied France, one needed false papers and two sets of visas: the first to cross the French-Belgian border, and the second, the demarcation line between occupied and unoccupied France. Crossing the latter often entailed—usually temporary—imprisonment.

There were a few other escape routes. In Brussels my friend Suzy Donner and her family got visas for the Belgian Congo. The price? Mr. Donner "gave" his lucrative film-leasing business to his collaborationist partner, who could provide the appropriate papers. The Donners left via southern France and Portugal.

As we searched for an escape, my mother decided that we should update our German passports. Hers was valid but lacked the mandated *J* and Jewish name. Since I now was fifteen, I needed a passport of my own.

My mother and I trudged to Brussels's German consulate. Notices threatening Jews with incarceration in a concentration camp if they failed to have their passports marked with a *J* were plastered all over the walls of the waiting room. I begged my mother to leave, but she insisted on seeing the consul. He saw us, listened to our requests, and told my astonished mother, "I need proof that you are Jewish and that the child is a full-Jew. After all, there are certain advantages to being Jewish." Surprisingly, we had some difficulties finding a document that clearly stated we were Jews. To this day, I don't know whether the consul was exceedingly pedantic or extremely kind when he advised us to claim we were non-Jews. In any case, my mother did not take the hint—if there was one—and decided to comply with the law.

Hitler hoped to be the undisputed master of Europe by the winter of 1940–41. In July 1940 he opened the Battle of Britain, whose ultimate objective was the occupation of the British Isles, which was separated from continental Europe by the narrow English Channel.

To begin with, German bombers and fighter planes were to pulverize England. The vastly outnumbered Royal Air Force (RAF) was the Luftwaffe's principal target, but major cities, especially London, were also bombed relentlessly in a campaign to demoralize the British people. The London blitz lasted three months, and by October 1940, 13,000 civilians were dead.

The Germans underestimated England's determination. The British knew that they were Europe's last bastion of freedom. As Winston Churchill said: "If we fail, then the whole world, including the United States, including all that we have known and cared for, will sink into the abyss of a new dark age."

Bombing civilian targets in addition to military ones dissipated the Germans' strength. The Luftwaffe lost the Battle of Britain as well as an immense number of planes and pilots. Hitler put his plan on hold until spring 1941. Few people realized it at the time, but the postponed invasion of England was the Third Reich's first defeat.

In Brussels, the gloom of the military debacle of the spring lifted a fraction. There were a few isolated cases of sabotage, such as cutting several high-voltage lines.

Everybody listened to the BBC. People greeted each other with Churchill's raised fingers, spelling the letter *V,* which stands for victory in English, *victoire* in French, and *Vrijheid* in Flemish. The BBC's evening broadcast, *London Here,* started with the first bars of Beethoven's Fifth Symphony—*dot, dot, dot, dash*—spelling *V* in Morse code.

A few clandestine mimeographed pages—later there would be a veritable underground press—told the population that the war was not "all over." One leaflet provided instructions on how to "unscramble" the German radio interference with the BBC broadcast. Actually, Belgians did not need any of the underground publications to be informed. Throughout the entire war, any news worth hearing traveled through the country like wildfire.

Individual Belgians established radio contact with Britain. From the very beginning, Belgium provided England with crucial information on German troop and train movement and other logistics information. Underground escape routes enabling volunteers, escaped prisoners, and downed airmen to reach Britain were organized and kept functional throughout the occupation. The illegals, accompanied by a guide, took the train from Brussels to Paris. The trip required two sets of false documents: Belgian papers to leave Belgium, and French papers to enter France. In Paris the fugitives were met by another guide, who assisted them across the demarcation line into unoccupied France. The next stops were villages near the Spanish border, from where robust Basque guides helped the escapees across the Pyrenees into Spain. The climb took a good twelve to fourteen hours. From Spain, England was reached by small boat. The trip was dangerous and expensive.

Once their courage returned, Belgians discreetly started displaying the national colors, especially on holidays. Some people sported small flags made from red, gold, and black ribbons; others simply wore color-coordinated clothes. Belgians also started tapping out the opening bars of Beethoven's Fifth Symphony whenever they felt like making a statement.

In Brussels the Germans continued to strut about in their polished black leather boots as if they owned the world. They flirted with all the girls, but had few takers. They ridiculed the British, Prime Minister Churchill, and the always optimistic BBC. Brussels was plastered with posters showing Churchill, surrounded by rubble, crooning into a BBC microphone: *"Tout va très bien Madame la Marquise . . ."* The lines referred to a popular song in which the butler phones his employer, telling her, "Everything is fine, my dear marquess, except that . . . the barn burned down, the horses escaped, the roof collapsed, the crops rotted." The butler kept piling up the disasters until it was clear that the marquess was destitute.

In spite of their setback in the Battle of Britain, the Fascists were gaining strength. In October 1940 the Italians invaded Greece. The Axis dominated most of the Mediterranean. Mussolini hoped to conquer the Suez Canal and the oil fields in the Middle East that supplied the British army with fuel.

If one managed to forget the imminent danger, life was pleasant enough. For the first time in her life, my mother was on her own, free of both her doting parents and her husband. My father had doled out a weekly household allowance, which had been generous in Germany and less so in Belgium. Whenever my mother wanted some extra clothes or books, she skimped on food. She had other ways of supplementing and stretching her budget. At the end of the week, she sometimes told Gaby and me to rifle through my father's pockets and collect forgotten small change.

Now mother was getting good prices for my father's machinery and the laboratory equipment and felt that we were well off, for a while at least. The money gave my mom a sense of power. Aware of my father's affair with Miss Botmann, she let herself enjoy Harry Salomon's devoted company; it was a balm to her wounded pride.

My mother had always felt especially close to Gaby, who like herself was the younger of two sisters. After our return from the coast, my mother asked Gaby to sleep in my father's vacant bed. I felt a bit left out.

In one way, my mother was the "boss," and indeed Gaby and I nicknamed her "chief." In another way, my mother and sister needed looking after. I knew that I had to grow up fast to help engineer our survival. I assumed some of the responsibility for the three of us and relished the importance and freedom it entailed.

I must have been born resourceful, instinctively relying on a mixture of common sense, perseverance, and sensitivity to others. I ran errands for the business, tracked down lost packages, obtained the necessary documents from a reluctant bureaucrat, fetched the food stamps from the town hall, or stood in line to get our food rations.

Though my mom relied on me heavily, she continued to treat me like a child and never willingly relinquished her authority. I still had a rigid bedtime and had to tell her where I went and what I did. Actually, it was a normal power struggle between an adolescent and her parent, but the perilous circumstances under which we lived made it special. My mother did not speak French as well as I did and often had to ask me the meaning of some words or phrases. She did not always understand what was acceptable behavior in Brussels and what was not. More than most adolescents, I realized that I could not always follow her advice, especially in crazy war-torn Europe, and I also was testing my own wings.

Because I knew how much she worried about our future, I never openly confronted her with my independence and did some things behind her back. I felt devious doing it, resenting having to pretend that I was "good" and "obedient," whatever that meant in these long-past times. My mom and I were often at odds.

Our differences were small, however, compared to our common goal of living through this catastrophe. My mother, my sister, and I were a strong team. Even today I identify readily with such a family constellation, believing that they are ideally suited for survival.

For me the La Panne expedition had yielded a social life. Gert, Pitt, Martin, Dédé, and I got together on weekends. We played Monopoly—Boardwalk, Marvin Gardens, Park Place, and other Atlantic City landmarks became familiar sites. Martin Salomon was a particularly enthusiastic player. Gert arranged excursions to the country, and occasionally, when we managed to come up with the money, Pitt bought tickets for concerts or the theater.

My mother did not give me much of an allowance, but I knew how she had increased her own budget in small ways and I followed her example. I took over the family's grocery shopping and kept some of the change. I felt very guilty and confessed my dishonesty to Elizabeth. I think now that I would have done more rather than tell my friends that I did not have enough money to participate in our outings. Taking another leaf from my mother's book, I hawked some of my possessions. The stores were bare, and I sold my embryonic stamp collection, my tennis racket, and my outgrown skates for a fair price.

I loved clothes. I cajoled my mother into having our dressmaker refashion some of her old dresses for me. In spite of strict instructions to the contrary, I borrowed my mother's clothes and jewelry, notably a red coral necklace that I loved dearly. Once, when I wore it to the theater, it broke. My friends and I scrambled for the beads during the rest of the performance, Pitt claiming later that we saw Bizet's *Pearl Fishers* instead of the Molière play we actually attended. I had the necklace restrung and replaced it before my mother missed it. When she wore it to the next get-together of our little gang, Pitt, tongue-in-cheek, exclaimed: "Oh, Mrs. Bamberger, I thought that necklace was broken."

After an uncomfortable silence, my mother claimed that she thought that the necklace felt funny when she put it on, but she fortunately dropped the matter.

My friendship with Elizabeth deepened. We fantasized less. After all, I now had a real love object: Gert Hirschland, about whom I could rave. Elizabeth too had found a platonic love: Eugène, who suffered from severe acne but made up for his unattractiveness by being a staunch Leftist.

I saw Gert as often as decorum permitted. Except for the one time that he gave me a red rose he had picked from a hedge while we talked, there was no sign of his returning my infatuation. I pressed the rose between the pages of my diary.

Fall had turned into winter. The coal left over from the previous winter was insufficient, and replacing it was difficult. In addition, each pail had to be carefully sifted so as to retrieve the gun I had hidden there when the war broke out. We finally recovered it and tossed it into a small stream. Gas for cooking was also in short supply and was available only for a few hours in the morning and evening. During that first winter, the grocery stores were empty and food was in very short supply. I was often hungry.

Belgian farms raised cattle and poultry. Other foods, especially grain products and animal feed, were imported. Lacking fodder, much of the livestock had to be slaughtered. As mandated by the Germans, farmers converted pastures into grain and potato fields. The changeover would take time, and our food supply was worse at the beginning of the occupation.

Each farmer was given a per-acre production quota. Most farmers had underreported their acreage and funneled their surplus production to the flourishing and essential black market.

Procuring sufficient food for the family was tedious, expensive, and fraught with mishaps. Once we bought a quart of olive oil on the black market. After we all developed diarrhea, we realized that we had been sold mineral oil. Stones were embedded into butter, flour was adulterated with fillers, cat meat masqueraded as rabbit. I often bicycled to the country to buy eggs, apples, and potatoes, which I transported strapped to the luggage rack of my bicycle. It was illegal to buy food on the black market, but nobody seemed to care.

Because Germans shipped Belgian coal to their homeland, coal too was in short supply. Anthracite bricks, tossed from moving railroad trains, ended up on the black market. Many people heated with wood, which was also sold clandestinely. Again, caution was advised. Wood, sold by weight, was sometimes so waterlogged that it refused to burn.

In spite of the oppressive atmosphere, my mother decided to celebrate New Years Eve. We invited our new friends: the Hirschlands, Salomons, and Beissingers. That morning I had my long-delayed first period. "You are a woman now," my mom said as she congratulated me.

Indeed I felt grown-up and chic as I donned her old fur jacket, with its enormous leopard-skin collar, and her knee-high leather boots before going off to do the shopping at the open-air market. On the way back, I fetched the two superb cakes my mother had ordered at our fancy neighborhood pastry shop.

"Since your father is in a camp, we really should not have a party," my mom said. "We also should not have spent the money, but . . ."

We welcomed our guests kind of guiltily, but forgot our misgivings when we ate the goodies and drank champagne contributed by Harry Salomon. Gert had written a skit entitled *The Memories of a Nurse-Maid's Wanderings Through Flanders.* His reminiscences dramatized our ill-fated expedition to the French border, when Gert—the nurse—pushed the baby carriage loaded with our suitcases through the Flemish countryside. All of our travel companions were at the party, except for Tante Lene, whose American visa had come through. I was happy that evening and ready for life to begin.

Chapter 5

The Net Tightens

I hate waiting. Yet that's all we seemed to be doing. During that long, first winter of the war, we waited for coal, for letters from my father, for food packages from Switzerland, for next month's ration stamps, for the next German decree, for the English to get stronger, for America to enter the war, and, most of all, for deciding what to do with ourselves.

Letters were our lifeline to the free world, yet we received few; and when we did, part of the text was blackened out by the censor. There was no direct communication with my grandparents and my aunt Erna in England. It took four months until we learned indirectly that Opa had died in October 1940. Our most reliable correspondents were our devoted Swiss cousins, who were in touch with my father and our family in America. The Ullmans felt responsible for our well-being. They sent money and food, and in 1941 they told us that they had managed to buy three visas for Ecuador. Nobody knew whether they were genuine.

News from Germany was grim. The harassment of the Jews continued. Elizabeth received anxious letters from her parents. Although the information was veiled, it transpired that her parents' medical practice was nonexistent and that they could shop for food only during a few hours each day. Worst of all, they expected to have to vacate their comfortable apartment.

After an exceedingly harsh winter, my father's letters from camp were more cheerful. He hoped that his visa for America would come through that spring. When he received it in April 1941, he was allowed to leave the camp. I cried when he wrote about going to a restaurant, eating from china plates, with real cutlery, at a table covered with a white cloth. My father was a fastidious man. My table manners had been a constant bone of contention. I realized how much he had hated the sloppy camp food served in mess kits.

My father managed to book passage on a New York–bound Portuguese ship. His letters, arriving in blacked-out Brussels, describing brightly lit Lisbon, were like from another world. Though he hardly mentioned it, we sensed his anxiety and sadness of leaving us behind in Europe. My father sailed in May, almost a year to the day since the Germans invaded Belgium. It was his good fortune, and ours, that he managed to escape then. Six weeks later the Germans decreed that no one with immediate family in Europe could leave France.

Mrs. Beissinger, her aged mother-in-law, and her young son finally decided to travel via the now well-established escape route to France. Despite reasonably good forged documents, the Beissingers were imprisoned as they crossed into unoccupied France. After much hassle they were released and reunited with Mr. Beissinger. Eventually the entire family escaped to Cuba.

My mother had opted against attempting the same journey, which in retrospect turned out to be a mistake. Not only could we have tried to go to Ecuador, but our U.S. visas had come up together with my father's. Because the U.S. consulate in occupied Belgium had closed, we had to appear at the American consulate in Perpignan, in unoccupied France. If we had been on the spot, we almost certainly would have been able to sail for America.

Confrontations between the Germans and the Belgian population escalated. In spite of General von Falkenhausen's desire to minimize friction, the Nazis embraced the Flemish-speaking Belgians and discriminated against those who spoke French. They hoped for the annexation of "Germanic" Flanders. Flemish prisoners of war continued to be released, while French-speaking soldiers remained in Germany as forced laborers. In spite of this partisanship, members of both ethnic groups took an active part in the ever-increasing Belgian resistance movement.

The persecution of the Jews in Belgium also escalated, though more slowly than in Germany and even in Holland. During the spring of 1941, it was decreed that Jewish children over the age of sixteen had to leave school by the end of the year.

By the end of May, we had to register our property and hand in our radios. Fortunately, my mother had already liquidated my father's business, and we had nothing to register. Our car had been requisitioned long ago. My mother sold our excellent shortwave radio and bought a cheap one that we handed in as instructed. Not having a radio made it even more difficult to know what was happening. Nobody trusted the German press, and now we were even deprived of the more reliable albeit overly optimistic BBC.

In many respects life continued to remain normal. Since my sixteenth birthday was that May, I left my beloved lyceé and abandoned my long-standing resolve to study chemistry. While waiting for God knows what, I tried to pick up some useful skills.

Vati had always suggested that regardless of what I was to study, I should learn typing and stenography. "That way a girl can always earn a living," he had said. I thus dutifully registered at the Institut Meysman, Belgium's most renowned secretarial school.

Learning stenography and typing was a dull and lonely pursuit. I had nothing in common with my older classmates, all of whom had concrete career plans. Because I was fluent in German, a language then in great demand, they realized that my chances for employment were excellent. They wondered why I never went on job interviews. Why did I bother to take the course?

My fellow students may even have considered me even more odd if I had told them that I felt I belonged in the lyceé and hoped to study chemistry so that I could help my father run the family business.

Attending the Institut Meysman did have some compensations. The school was located in the center of old Brussels. Sainte Gudule, the city's imposing Gothic cathedral, was across the street. I visited it occasionally. The mixed messages of my religious upbringing had endowed me with respect for all faiths.

As I entered the enormous cathedral, I felt safe. I did not pray but looked reverently and sheepishly at the statues of Sainte Gudule and Saint

Michel, Brussels's twin patron saints. I fervently hoped that if they had any power they might consider protecting my family.

The spirit of the Grande Place with its spectacular Gothic town hall and the medieval guild houses was close to my heart. The square was always at the center of Belgium's long struggle for independence and religious freedom. During the Spanish occupation four centuries earlier, Philip II ordered the public execution of the counts of Egmont and Hoorn on the Grande Place.

I often walked all the way home from school, a distance of some thirty minutes. Sometimes I passed through the elegant parts of town, looking at the expensive clothes displayed in the fancy shops. I carefully crossed the Boulevard de la Toison d'Or, remembering the truck that had mowed me down. Sometimes I walked through the Rue Haute, a narrow street that had been the commercial hub of old Brussels. The painter Pieter Brueghel, who depicted the everyday life of the comfortable middle class during the sixteenth century, was buried in the church heading the street. At that time there had already been Jews in Brussels. One street was still called Rue des Juifs. During World War II, the Rue Haute was the center of a thriving black market. The shops openly displayed coffee, ham, butter, chocolate, soap, and white bread—all of which had disappeared from ordinary groceries. My mouth watered as I passed.

The courses at the Institut Meysman filled only half my day. I doubted that I would ever be a top-notch secretary. My spelling was atrocious, and I was inconsistent at such exacting tasks as formatting letters. I wanted to learn another trade.

I had always admired the hats displayed in a small millinery shop near my house. One day I went inside and asked the owner whether she could use an apprentice. Suzy Tamineau, a blue-eyed young woman, was surprised by the request but said she would give me a try.

From then on I spent my afternoons in her workshop, a small apartment located above her shop. Suzy let me baste, line the crown of the hats with grosgrain ribbon, and steam and varnish the finished products. Sometimes she even allowed me to stretch a hard-to-come-by new felt cone over a wooden hat form.

When I was not helping Suzy, I made hats for my mother, myself, my friends, or my sister. It was difficult to buy felt, but my mother had an ample supply of old hats that I remodeled. That year fashion dictated minuscule hats perched on the forehead. My artistic creativity, as always, exceeded my technical know-how. I made some pretty hats and even managed to sell some to another millinery store. This was the first money I ever made.

My real education at Suzy's, however, had nothing to do with hats. I listened endlessly to stories about her former lovers, her current fiancé—a penniless painter called Willy—sex, loyalty, fidelity, mistresses, and love triangles.

Suzy's family was fascinating. There were aunts who left the church and married, and a cousin who got pregnant out of wedlock. There was Brother Raymond, her father's best friend, who became addicted to movies when he was an official film censor for the Catholic church. Then he committed some offense or other and was demoted to being a provincial prison chaplain. When he came to Brussels, he visited the Tamineaus, borrowed a suit from Suzy's father, and went to the movies.

My favorite stories concerned Suzy's success as a woman. I vicariously enjoyed the ball at which her escort bought the flower vendor's entire stock of violets because their color matched Suzy's eyes. I told Suzy about my family, Gert, and Miss Botmann. The afternoons passed quickly.

My love affair with Gert was over before it got off the ground. In 1941 Gert met Roli Bernheim and fell in love. Roli was everything I was not. She had poise, good looks, smashing clothes, and, most of all, considered herself irresistible. She disliked the outdoors, hiking, and camping, and it surprised me how quickly she domesticated Gert.

I wondered how many people knew how desperately I had wanted to be Gert's girlfriend and perhaps even his wife. Had I made a fool of myself? I was sad and felt humiliated. Because I continued to see Gert, Roli, Pitt, and Martin, I pretended that I did not give a damn. I burned the diary I had been keeping and the pressed rose Gert had given me.

It was good to share these stories with Suzy, whose love life had so many ups and downs. She too must have enjoyed my company; I cannot imagine that my clumsy sewing was of great help.

Since I no longer attended the lycée, it was more difficult to spend time with Elizabeth. My friend became an increasingly militant Marxist and had little patience for my more bourgeois aspirations. It was not, however, attachment to the material comforts that made me hesitate joining her cause. I suspected that the Communists were opportunists who always managed to explain every immoral action by saying that the end justifies the means. On the other hand, the Communists I knew were trustworthy friends, genuinely devoted to the defeat of Fascism. My loyalty thus continued to be split. The bonds that united Elizabeth and me were much stronger than our differences. Our bleak reality grew bleaker by the month.

In August 1941 the Germans imposed an 8 P.M. to 7 A.M. curfew for Jews. Because the Brussels police force did not cooperate with the Germans, the curfew was not really enforceable. Nevertheless we felt uncomfortable being out after eight o'clock, and thus complied with the regulation.

I had gotten hold of a copy of *Gone With the Wind,* and I could not put it down; I read long past my bedtime. The story of the American Civil War, the customs of the old South, and the trials and tribulations of Scarlett O'Hara captivated me completely. I envied Scarlett's popularity, but even more admired her resilience in the face of disaster. I copied the last lines of the book and carried them with me:

"I won't think of it now," she thought grimly ". . . I'll go home to Tara tomorrow. . . ." She had gone to Tara once in fear and defeat and she had emerged from its sheltering walls strong and armed for victory. What she had done once, somehow—please God, she could do again! How, she did not know. . . . All she wanted was a breathing space in which to hurt, a quiet place to lick her wounds, a haven in which to plan her campaign. . . .

"With the spirit of her people who would not know defeat, even when it stared them in the face, she raised her chin. She could get Rhett back. She knew she could. There had never been a man she couldn't get, once she set her mind upon him."

I had no Tara, nor had I yet conquered any man, but I took comfort from Scarlett's guts, determination, and courage. Elizabeth dismissed *Gone With the Wind* as trash and wondered how anyone could spend any sympathy on the plight of plantation and slave owners.

The Axis continued to enlarge its domain. In April 1941 the Nazis decided to help the Italians in Greece. Within two weeks the country surrendered and the British army left. We lost Crete, and Yugoslavia fell during that same offensive. The Mediterranean, traditionally a British stronghold, was more threatened than ever.

On June 22, 1941, on the one-hundred-twenty-ninth anniversary of Napoleon's ill-fated invasion, the Germans attacked Soviet Russia. This treacherous violation of their nonaggression treaty was not surprising. Hitler considered the Russians "subhuman" and unfit to be part of his new world order.

I would have liked to listen to Mademoiselle Feytmans's commentaries. Could Hitler succeed where Napoleon had failed? Initially, in 1812, Napoleon's armies were victorious. Now the Russians buckled under the impact of the German army, reinforced by Hungarians, Romanians, Finns, and other traditional Russian enemies. The Germans advanced rapidly, overrunning Russia's fertile lands and occupying the industrialized western portion of the republic. They hoped to take Moscow by August and got within thirty miles of the capital. The Russians proved tougher than the Germans expected. By October 1941 the advance slackened, and by November it came to a halt.

As in Napoleon's time, winter came early. The telescopic sights of the German tanks frosted over and became useless. The German army had neither antifreeze for its vehicles nor warm clothing for its soldiers. Yet Hitler insisted on an attack on Moscow. At tremendous cost the Germans fought their way into the outskirts of the Russian capital. Stalin's army held fast and, on December 6, even counterattacked. Then both armies bedded down for the long Russian winter.

The Germans treated their former allies harshly. Some war prisoners and civilians were executed on the spot; others were shipped to forced-labor camps. When this became known, the Russians realized that they were fighting for their survival and redoubled their efforts.

Until the Germans invaded Russia, the Belgian Communists lay low, declaring that World War II was "a capitalist conflict." Now they were in the forefront of the resistance, some contributing what they had learned duing the Spanish Civil War. Engineers trained at the Free University of Brussels manufactured explosive devices and used them to blow up German trucks. Initially, the raw materials used for the manufacture were stolen, then supplies were parachuted in by the British. The Communists linked up with other underground organizations. Sabotage, as well as the execution of individual Fascists, collaborators, and Germans, increased sharply, as did retaliation by the enemy.

Some members of the resistance were known, and the Gestapo posted big "wanted" ads throughout Belgium. Information leading to arrest was rewarded by a half million Belgian francs. Fortunately, the tidy sum had few takers. Nevertheless there were arrests. In Brussels the newly apprehended were interrogated and tortured at the Gestapo headquarters, located on the Avenue Louise, in the hope that they would inform on others. After that, prisoners were transferred to Saint Gilles, the local prison, and to Breendonck, Belgium's especially deadly concentration camp.

In spite of von Falkenhausen's plea for leniency, the Germans took hostages. Sometimes these innocent bystanders were simply murdered in their homes; sometimes they were arrested and executed. In Brussels execution took place at the Tir National Rifle Range.

The population was incensed at these reprisals. The funerals of victims turned into such massive demonstrations that the Germans often prohibited funeral masses and processions.

As the occupation progressed, resistance to the Germans became a mass movement. Without belonging to an organized group, countless individuals took it upon themselves to come to the rescue of those in distress. None of the people who saved my mother, my sister, or myself belonged to any group, nor had they planned to take an active part in defeating the Germans. When given the opportunity to save someone's life, they did, even though by the very act they put themselves and their family at enormous risk.

To occupied Europe's distress, the United States and its vast resources remained neutral. History remembers the surprise attack on Pearl Harbor—December 7, 1941—as a day of infamy. In Brussels we rejoiced when the BBC announced that "as a consequence of the Japanese attack, a state of war exists between Japan and the United States." By December 11, Germany and Italy declared war on the United States.

I never doubted that the Germans would lose the war. The end of the conflict, however, was far in the future, and the danger to those trapped in continental Europe increased steadily.

Chapter 6

The Yellow Star

The Germans were busy fighting in the East, West, and in Africa. Still they were ready to intensify their persecution of Jews. In November 1941 the Germans forced the Jewish community to form the Association des Juifs, which was to help ready Jews for deportation. Aside from having registered the Jews in October 1940, the Belgian authorities refused to participate in the Germans "war against the Jews." On the contrary, in Brussels the Belgian officials were exceedingly helpful to the Jews, and their contribution to their ultimate survival cannot be overestimated. Matters were different in Antwerp, where the predominantly Flemish population was anti-Semitic.

During the Middle Ages, Jews had had to identify themselves by wearing a pointed yellow hat. In May 1942 the Germans issued ugly swatches of yellow cloth imprinted with a Star of David and the word *Juif.* When in public we had to wear the emblem on our outer garment.

I was more mortified than mad. It had always been exceedingly important to me to blend in with my surroundings. I found it unbearable to be openly identified as being different. At first I refused to wear the damn star. When my mother insisted, I sewed it onto my dresses and hid it under a coat, jacket, or scarf. Luckily, I was never challenged.

I had graduated from secretarial school in the spring of 1942 and was bored and at loose ends. I was already seventeen years old and my life was ticking away! I still spent my afternoons making hats at Suzy's. In my unending quest for education, I registered for an evening Spanish class, given free at the Brussels South American Institute. To get home before curfew, I sneaked out before the class was over. Actually, I rarely made it home in time and at my streetcar stop often ran into a classmate who had stayed until the end. "Ha," he said smirking from ear to ear, "trying to get home in time for the curfew?" How I hated him. Much later I discovered that he too was Jewish and simply ignored the regulation. The Nazis finally rescinded our German citizenship, which did not matter since our "father-land" had abandoned us long ago.

One of our friends—a German Gentile woman married to a German Jewish man—had a nephew serving in the German army. He visited his aunt regularly and told her that in Germany Jews were being evicted from their homes and "resettled" in Eastern Europe. Since such developments eventu-ally arrived in Belgium, we too expected to be "resettled."

By then the "Final Solution," as the Nazis dubbed their extermination plan, had been worked out. Jews from all over Europe were shipped to Eastern Europe and awaited extermination.

Unbeknownst to the public, von Falkenhausen had been ordered by Heinrich Himmler and Adolf Eichmann, the chief architects of the "Final Solution," to "deliver" twenty thousand Jews living in Belgium by the end of August. The requested twenty thousand were foreign nationals. Belgian Jews were exempted for the time being.

We were notified, by mail, that we had to report to a camp in the nearby town of Malines on August 15, 1942. The letter, ostensibly sent by the Asso-ciation des Juifs and signed by the rabbi, carefully stated that ours was to be a labor camp and that it would be "safe to go," whatever that meant. The letter urged us to comply. It said that if we did not report to the camp, other Jews would have to "do our share of the work." Most of our friends, includ-ing the Hirschlands and Salomons, received similar notices.

My mother decided right away not to go to Malines. A sense of forebod-ing surrounded the camps that were springing up in Eastern Europe. Rumors circulated. One had it that the Germans were sending young Jewish girls to brothels on the Eastern Front. By now I was a ripe, busty teenager and would be a prime candidate for such an establishment. Also, since my twelve-year-old sister was still a child, my mother doubted that we really would be sent to a labor camp.

None of our close friends complied with the German summons. One exception was David Seligman. He had left Germany only in 1939, his Gentile wife having divorced him. Alone and destitute, this sweet forty-five-year-old man befriended us. He was extremely grateful to my mother for her hospitality and was especially fond of my young sister. In spite of my mother's entreaties, David left for Malines. We never heard of him again.

We had a few weeks to "disappear" and weighed various options. Briefly, my mother considered marrying me off to a non-Jew. Such paper marriages were for sale and afforded some protection for the entire family. My mother fortunately abandoned this plan and decided that we should go into hiding instead.

Because living illegally would be expensive, my mother intensified her efforts to turn our possessions into cash. She found buyers for the six matched red oak bookcases, the massive dining room furniture, the overstuffed velvet armchairs, my parents' elegant custom-made Bauhaus bedroom set, the antique armoire she had received as a bride, the embroidered linen tablecloths and sheets, the silver flatware for twenty-four, the endless silver platters, the Rosenthal china, the enormous George Grosz oil painting that had hung in the wintergarden in our big house in Hanover, my father's collection of apothecary jars, her art books, and many other treasures. She went about the liquidation cheerfully, quoting her best friend, Else, who allegedly preached "not to make one's happiness hostage to material possessions." Some furniture, artwork, silver, books, and other items that my mother was particularly fond of were stored with friends.

It was much more difficult to dispose of ourselves. Fortunately, we were the protégées of René Fuss, Harry Salomon's lawyer. Obtaining false identity papers was the first order of business. Fuss bought me a blank green Belgian identity card, stolen from the town hall in Liège. Fuss and I filled it out in the name of "Suzanne Berger," a name so close to my real one that it did not matter if I turned around or flinched when someone called me Bamberger. We looked in the phone book for an address, made up a birth date, parents, and other details. Somebody else then affixed my picture to the card and stamped it with the appropriate seal. I was legal.

My mother thought that I would look less Jewish if my hair were not black. I had it bleached at the beauty parlor. The peroxide turned it a beautiful shade of titian-red. I do not know if I looked less Jewish, but my curly mane of red hair certainly was very conspicuous.

For a small sum of money, the Hirschlands' cleaning woman agreed to give her identity card to my mother. Then the woman went to the town hall, claiming that she had lost her identity card and needed a duplicate. René Fuss arranged to have my mother's photograph substituted for that of the legal owner. My mother's name henceforth was Josephine Remy Van den Einde. She never learned to say "Van den Einde" and called herself Madame Josephine Remy. For her this name held some magic, as her beloved father's name had been Joseph. Gaby, being under fifteen, did not need any identification papers.

We knew that our false papers would not withstand close scrutiny. A check with the town hall in Liège would immediately indicate that there was no record for a Suzanne Berger. A check on Madame Van den Einde's identity card would show the issue of a duplicate. Better false papers were harder to obtain and also cost much more money.

We also looked for shelter. My friend Suzy let us move into the workroom above the millinery store. We promised to stay only a few days. Because I was my mother's gravest concern, I moved there on August 5. I was alone in the studio when a plumber showed up. After he had fixed the sink, he suggested that we make love. I was terrified. Fortunately, he did not insist.

I did not stay at Suzy's for long. One of the groups that took an active part in hiding the Jews were the teachers. Thus Madame de Backer, Gaby's former teacher, let it be known that she was trying to place a Jewish teenager. The request reached the principal of the school at which Nelly Wiame taught. She was about to have her first baby. Aware of Nelly's liberal leanings, the principal told her about me, and soon thereafter I was invited to visit the young couple. Jean and Nelly Wiame decided that I would do, and within days I became their "mother's helper."

Before assuming my job, I bid good-bye to the Hollenders. They also had decided to "vanish." Elizabeth and I said little and did not exchange addresses. We did not want the burden of knowing where the other was. The Gestapo often tortured those it arrested and forced them to reveal the hiding places of their family and friends. It was both wise and proper wartime etiquette to avoid questioning others about what they chose to do.

♦

After I left for the Wiames, my mother and Gaby moved into Suzy's workroom. When Suzy told her brother that she was sheltering Jews, he got frightened and insisted that Suzy get rid of my mother and sister immediately. Suzy complied, but she contacted Brother Raymond—the film buff.

At one time during his complicated career in the Catholic church, Brother Raymond had served as parish priest in the village of Baasrode. There he had befriended the Vinckes, whom he now asked to shelter my sister.

Baasrode is in the Flemish-speaking part of Belgium. Because of the Germans' successful courtship of the Flemish population, hiding there was less safe than hiding in Brussels. Moreover, the Vinckes were already suspect. Joseph Vincke, the chief breadwinner of the family, had been a member of the resistance. He was denounced and deported to Germany, leaving behind his wife, Romanie, his elderly parents, and three young children. In spite of their misfortune, the Vinckes welcomed Gaby.

When my sister arrived, the neighbors were told that Gaby was too sick to attend school and might benefit from a prolonged stay in the relatively fresh country air of Baasrode. Gaby looked healthy. Fortunately, she fainted in church during the first Sunday the Vinckes took her there, which lent some credence to the story.

Perhaps the Vinckes' neighbors really believed that my sister was ill; perhaps they felt that the family needed Gaby's boarding fee; perhaps they were kind. The money my mother paid for Gaby's keep certainly bolstered the Vinckes' income, but it was only a small part of the bargain. The Vinckes became so attached to my sister that they would have kept her even if my mother had been unable to pay.

Brother Raymond also talked to Dominick and Delphine Bellins, cousins of the Vinckes. They lived in a small, primitive house with outdoor plumbing and agreed to rent my mother a room.

The Bellins too enjoyed the rent money, but again, finances were only a small part of the deal. Delphine, an ex-nun, had broken her vows when she married and felt her salvation was threatened. She hoped that helping my mother would increase her credit in heaven. Her chances of salvation would be even greater were she to convert my mother to Catholicism. Delphine soon gave up on my mother's soul, but the family was delighted by my mother, who was so unlike anyone they had ever met.

♦

I arrived at Jean and Nelly Wiame's home on August 10, 1942. They lived in an isolated white stucco house in Auderghem, another of Brussels's many boroughs. Their small flat was on the first floor.

Jean and Nelly were in their late twenties. They had met at the university and married the day the Germans invaded Belgium. Jean then was in the Belgian army. Nelly intended to keep up with him by fleeing to France like the rest of us. As it was, Jean was discharged and returned to Brussels long before Nelly did. The due date of their baby was October, only two months hence.

The French-speaking Free University of Brussels is nonsectarian. It was founded to oppose the dominance of the Catholic church. Now many of its students had leftist leanings. After the German invasion, teaching activities continued unhampered, even though the university was forced to accept some German exchange professors. In November 1941, however, when the German authorities insisted that the university appoint three pro-German activists to its board, the governors of the university ordered it closed.

The Wiames, whose studies and careers were temporarily halted, changed employment. Jean worked at a technical school—the Institut de Fermentation—and Nelly taught zoology at one of Brussels's best high schools.

Meeting the Wiames was a totally new experience for me. Jean, the son of blue-collar workers, had managed to rise above his background through his own hard work and intellectual gifts. Such a feat was then very rare in Europe. I am not sure that he ever felt quite at ease in his new milieu. Nelly's parents, on the other hand, were squarely middle class. Her father, a Swiss businessman, had come to Belgium in 1905 and founded the Etablissement Wanner, a successful cork business that designed and manufactured stoppers and packing materials for bottles and barrels. When old Mr. Altorfer died in 1939, he was a wealthy man. Nelly's mother, a determined middle-aged battle-axe, ran the business, her household, and her children with an iron fist. She disapproved heartily of her unconventional son-in-law, always pointing out his careless demeanor, tardiness at mealtime, and poor manners.

I was unaware of such tensions when I moved in with Jean and Nelly. My bosses were much in love. I was fascinated by their devotion to each other, the intellectual atmosphere of their house, their friends, their books, their conversation, the pictures on their walls, the biological specimens drying on the radiators, their pets, and their leftist political views. I knew that if I survived the war I wanted a life like theirs.

By the end of August my mother, my sister, and I were safely hidden. For us that meant living normally and openly with false identity cards. As the occupation dragged on, the Germans organized an increasing number of raids on streetcars and trains, and in movie houses and other public places at which one had to show an identity card. These spot checks were designed to catch resistance workers transporting arms, underground news-papers, or forged documents; draft dodgers; Jews; and other illegals. It was prudent to minimize such exposures. My mother urged me to stay close to home, to avoid public places and trips downtown. Being young and feeling immortal, I did not listen to her and exposed myself to danger unnecessar-ily. I even experienced a certain thrill when the Germans examined my false papers during such raids.

In one's immediate neighborhood, one's safety depended on the kind-ness of the cop on the beat. By law he had to check that any new resident of his district registered with the local town hall. During the war, members of the Belgian police, doubtlessly aware of who lived where, usually looked the other way.

We had vacated our apartment just in time. From the beginning of August until the end of October, the Germans assembled seventeen hun-dred Jews, representing two-thirds of the total deported from Belgium dur-ing the entire occupation! Initially, this number consisted mostly of Jews who, like our friend David Seligman, had reported to Malines. When the number of Jews who showed up voluntarily fell markedly short of the twenty-thousand requested, the Germans started raiding Jewish neighborhoods in Antwerp and Brussels.

These mass arrests produced such vigorous protests from the Belgian authorities that large-scale operations were discontinued in Belgium. From then on the Germans concentrated on arresting individual Jews. A reward was offered to anyone betraying Jews in hiding. In addition, small German units patrolled the streets of big cities, pouncing on anyone looking Jewish or behaving in a suspicious manner. The patrols included Jewish informers. In Brussels the best known of these were known only as "Jacques" and "Adler."

◆

During the early weeks of my stay at the Wiames', I thought that I was about to come down with tonsillitis. Actually, my throat hurt because I constantly held back tears. I was very homesick.

My liberal views did not help. I hated being a servant. The realizations that the job was saving my life and that I shared in the Wiames' social life did not mean a thing. I had listened long enough to Elizabeth, however, to absorb some of her disdain for "bourgeois feelings," so, in addition to being miserable, I was ashamed of the way I felt.

I was terrible at keeping house. Jean and Nelly went off to work early in the morning, six days a week. It was up to me to clean the house, make the beds, stuff the elaborate stove with sawdust, make soup from scraps, feed the animals, do the wash, iron the sheets, and tend to endless other chores. After attending to the drudgery, I escaped my boring routine by selecting one of the many books from the shelves that lined every wall of the house.

My favorites were novels, especially the endless French romans-fleuves written by Romain Rolland, Roger Martin du Gard, and Jules Romains. I also devoured works by André Malraux, André Gide, Henri Barbusse, and Stefan Zweig. Many of these books dealt with World War I. They personalized the terror of the trenches; the senseless slaughter of men by their fellowmen; the hopelessness, the despair, the heartache of losing friends; and the belief that the horror of the war would at the very least result in a permanent, everlasting peace. Though these books dealt with another war and another time, they echoed my own distress and anguish. Often the world they described became more real to me than the one I lived in.

No wonder the house was a mess! I returned to my household duties shortly before Jean and Nelly came home and braced myself for Nelly's comments on the state of the kitchen.

I developed a little ritual to help me go to sleep. I sat on the top step of the stairs, in complete darkness. In my thoughts I went home. I slowly opened the front door of our apartment, glanced in the kitchen on the right as I passed it, and looked at my mother reading in the living room. She sat on one of the fat, upholstered black velvet chairs. Then I turned sharply right and went down the hall to my room. This made my feel better.

My chronic throatache disappeared one Saturday afternoon when a tall, slender, dark-haired "older" man came to the kitchen as I was struggling with the carrots and potatoes for the soup.

"You must be Suzanne," he said, "I am Emile, Nelly's brother. How are you doing?"

Not since I had left my home had anyone asked how I felt about my change from "daughter of the house" to *bonne à tout faire* to (general maid). Emile had asked about me. He cared.

At thirty-two, Emile was almost twice my age. He too had gone to Brussels' magic university, earning a degree in engineering. As the only male heir of a thriving enterprise, it was unthinkable for Emile to abandon the family business. As a matter of fact, he had assumed the directorship of the cork factory a few years earlier after the elder Altorfer had died.

Even though Emile did not openly rebel against being the heir and head of a successful commercial operation, engineering and the cork business were not his chief interest. He and his wife, Mariette, believed that Communism was the answer to mankind's ills.

It was Emile's personal concern and manner that had captivated me that afternoon, not his, now-familiar Communist views. These reminded me of Elizabeth, however, and revived my personal doubts about Communism. I believed that my objections would vanish once I really understood its nature. I planned to read *Das Kapital*—the book by Marx and Engels that forms the basis of this political system. I hoped that this would help me become a true believer.

I now doubt that doing this homework would have made me a convert. Even then I had an innate distrust of all dogma, of blind, unquestioning adherence to some faith or other—no matter how good the theory sounded. I was witnessing the destruction that could be wrought by ideas. I saw well-meaning people, even personal friends, forsake their own judgment and behave in disgusting ways, because the Nazis sanctioned or dictated such actions. I remembered our neighbor in Hanover, the minister of the local church, who no longer greeted me because I was Jewish; the birthday parties I was no longer invited to; the boys who had chased me and my dog.

On the other hand, it was very hard *not* to be a Communist. The Marxist principle *to each according to his need* appealed to my sense of justice, and the valiant fight put up by the Communists in Spain, Italy, and elsewhere was the only beacon of hope for those hunted by the Fascists. My objections to Communism seemed to crumble when I met Emile.

Emile must have been an important man in the Belgian underground.

He had decided that it was too risky for him to live at home in the apartment he shared with Mariette and their four-year-old daughter, Annie. During the winter and spring of 1942-43, he spent one or two nights a week at his sister's house in Auderghem. He showed up, always unannounced, in time to eat the dinner I prepared, discussing the war, politics, news, books, and other matters with Jean and Nelly.

Sometimes Gert Ochinsky, a friend of Jean and Nelly's, also showed up; he was a German Jewish refugee like myself. When Gert and Emile came the same night, the illegals outnumbered the legals. As Nelly said, with black humor, it did not matter whether one was shot for three rather than for two.

It was extraordinarily exciting for me to have three "older men" to play with, and I managed to entice them to horse around. Not having had much physical contact with boys since my elementary school days in Hanover, I had decided that the physical superiority of the male sex was purely a myth. Jean, Gert, and Emile were always ready to show me that my beliefs were wrong. I was both provocative and naive. Once, when Nelly had gone off to visit an aunt, Jean gently asked me whether we should spend the night together.

I was unaware that I had started to bloom. One evening I sat at Jean's desk, deeply engrossed in a book, unaware that darkness had turned the window into a shining mirror. When I looked up, an unknown, appealing young woman faced me. She smiled when I smiled. She too hastily got up to pull the curtains before the local cop complained about the noncompliance with the blackout. The girl was me! Did I look that good? From then on, coming upon a mirror unexpectedly became a great source of comfort.

Still I remained rather oblivious to my own attractiveness, and this may have added to my charm. I was also completely inexperienced, and my innocence was so obvious that it somehow protected me when I found myself in a risky situation.

The evenings that Emile spent at the Wiames' house compensated in large part for the long, boring days filled with the tedium of wartime housekeeping. I convinced myself that I was finally a true Communist. I attributed my former reluctance to being a spoiled brat.

Instead of Marx and Engels, however, I continued to devour books retelling World War I or French classics by Stendhal, Balzac, and Daudet.

As I dusted the living room or scrubbed the pots, I fantasized. I daydreamed of joining the resistance, being an effective spy, saving the lives of five partisans—because a German general was overwhelmed by my charms and my brains.

I fantasized about Emile most of all. My prudish soul had to find excuses for making love to a married man. I had constructed a whole series of unlikely plots, such as being incarcerated with Emile, without food or hope of salvation. These circumstances provided license to succumb to our desire.

The reality of my life was quite different, but in many ways it was as absurd. I worked so hard. There were the everyday chores of shopping for the grown-ups, the guests, and Pirou, the dog. Then there was the axolotl, a primitive creature that subsisted on freshly caught wiggly worms. I fished for these in the sluggish stream that passed by the house. I tried to keep the house in order and heated water to wash the floors and, only once a week, ourselves. I dragged up coal and sawdust from the cellar to feed the stoves that kept us warm.

But this was only part of the reality. I also knew that the Germans could pick me up any day and deport me to the terrifying East. In 1942-43 nobody as yet knew what took place in the camps, but being arrested was equated with certain doom.

Though I was happy and cheerful during the days, I had the most frightening recurring nightmare. A boatman, much like Charon who, in Greek mythology, ferried the dead to the Underworld, rowed me to a small island. I climbed out of the boat and started to wander among bare trees. Skeletons clung to the trees with bare hands and feet. The skeletons were not dead, but alive. One of them was Gert Ochinsky. He leered and tried to grab me with his bony fingers. The images were so vivid that I used to awake with a scream, not daring to go back to sleep.

In October 1942, a week before the expected birth of her baby, Nelly moved back to her mother's well-run home in Scheut. Because of Emile and Mariette's involvement with the resistance, Nelly felt that the house might be under surveillance, and she asked me to temporarily find other quarters.

On my behalf, Harry Salomon approached Bets and Hein Vorwinden, long-standing customers of his once-thriving wine business. The Vorwindens agreed to shelter me for a month or two until I could safely return to the

Wiames. This was extremely courageous and generous on their part, because Tante Bets, as I was to call her, and Lientje and Ben, the two children from her first marriage, were Jewish.

The Vorwindens were Dutch. A few years earlier, when Hein Vorwinden retired from his coffee-importing business, they had moved from Rotterdam to Brussels, because life in Belgium was inexpensive and pleasant. Like the Wiames, the Vorwindens lived in Auderghem, and it took me seven minutes to walk from one house to the other.

The Vorwindens' house was a spacious Victorian-type villa with a substantial garden. It was at the end of a street and abutted a large park, the Parc de Woluvé. The house was so isolated that one had the feeling of being in the country. The Vorwindens' furniture reflected past bourgeois splendor: worn Oriental rugs, faded brocade upholstery, and shredded silk drapes.

Monsieur Vorwinden—Oom Hein to me—was in his seventies and appeared unbelievably old. During his long life, he had engaged in gentlemanly upper-middle-class pursuits such as hunting, fishing, riding, sharpshooting, croquet, and mah-jong. He must have been very good at these, because his house overflowed with trophies, mostly intricate Meissen figurines. I dutifully dusted these every day. There were ninety-six of them.

By the time I met him, Oom Hein no longer participated in competitions. He spent much of his time playing endless games of solitaire. His favorite one was "the Napoleon," played with two decks of cards. When he won he was happy. Most often, however, he lost. When the cards looked bad, he kept muttering in Dutch, *"Het loopt mis* [it runs afoul]."

Chess was another passion. Because he had no friends, Oom Hein played with an imaginary partner. Once he took me on. Not taking me very seriously, he played carelessly and I almost checkmated him. This one-time success left me with a sense of exhilaration. We seldom played after that.

It was Tante Bets who wielded the power in the house. She was a scrawny woman of forty-five. A tightly woven net imprisoned her hair, and her pinched lips never smiled. Tante Bets was also Dutch, but her background was both more humble and more intellectual.

The Vorwindens kept very much to themselves; they had no friends and they established links with neither a church nor a synagogue. When Jews had to register at the local town hall, Tante Bets simply ignored the order, hoping that nobody would come to investigate. She worried about her beloved brother, however, and his five children who lived in Holland.

At first Tante Bets welcomed me as a daughter. Dusting was about the only household work that was proper for me to do. All the cooking and real cleaning was done by Bertha, a woman of about fifty.

I was to occupy my time as befitted a young lady: sewing, reading, knitting, taking music and foreign-language lessons, and looking for a suitable husband. I could not attend to any of these, but I dutifully struggled through the English original of *The Scarlet Pimpernel*, written by the Baroness Emmuska Orczy. Given the times, the book, which recounts the adventures of the British aristocrat who saved French noblemen from the guillotine during the French Revolution, was uplifting.

My room was on the third floor of the house, next to the attic, used only for storing a whole bushel of onions. The room had a small terrace from which I had an unobstructed view of the gardens that surrounded the neighborhood and of the adjacent park. My quarters were very cold that winter, but I loved the privacy they offered.

Life at the Vorwindens was very rigid. Bertha served breakfast, lunch, and dinner punctually, and there never was any conversation during mealtime. Whenever somebody—often me—talked during the meal, Tante Bets declared, *"Eten en zweijgen* [eat and shut up]." This admonition might not have been so difficult to follow had there been enough to eat.

For adults the official rations provided less than fourteen hundred calories a day, one-third less than the absolute minimum. Growing adolescents like me required more. Those who could afford it bought food on the black market. The price of food was exorbitant. A loaf of white bread cost 50 francs instead of the official 1.50; a stick of butter cost 80 francs instead of 4; sugar was a bargain at 20 francs a pound instead of less than 2. But coffee was the clincher—it retailed at 1 franc per bean. There were set black-market prices for meat, eggs, shortening, chocolate, and everything else one's heart desired. One of my favorite fantasies was deciding whether I would prefer "pigging out" on red meat or chocolate.

Neither was in the cards. The Vorwindens had decided *not* to buy any food on the black market, so we made do with the skimpy rations. Breakfast and dinner consisted of precounted slices of foul-smelling, sticky, ration bread. On this we spread Bovril—a concentrated soup base available without food stamps. Oom Hein, as a senior citizen, and the children, who were under sixteen, received food supplements. Thus only Tante Bets and I had to make do with the regular meager fare provided by food stamps.

When we sat down to eat, I was famished and rapidly wolfed down my bread. Then, still hungry, I watched during the endless hour it took the others to finish their more-appealing fare. Sometimes I managed to eat slowly, dissecting my bread with knife and fork, adjusting my rate to that of Tante Bets. Nevertheless, I always finished first.

I enjoyed my stay at the Vorwindens. The older-sister role I played was quite familiar. I was relieved, however, when Nelly decided to return to her own home and I could resume my job.

The Vorwindens and I remained friends. Since their house was only a short walk from the Wiames', I visited regularly, even spending an occasional weekend. It was during one of these weekends that I would start keeping a diary.

Engagement of my parents: Gretel Schwarzhaupt (Mutti, Maman) and
Hugo Bamberger (Vati) in Nurenberg, Germany. 1923.

Our house in
Hanover, Germany.
The Eilenriede,
a large forest, was
on the opposite side
of the street.

Part of my class at the Rudolf Steiner school in Hanover. Dark-haired Ruth-Iris Freudenthal is standing to the right of the teacher. Grete Stinnis, the staunch Nazi, stands on the teacher's left. I am in the back row, the third child from the right. Hans Pessler, to whom I gave foreign stamps from my father's factory, is the fourth boy from the left in the front row.

Gaby and me shortly before we left Germany. 1938.

My parents and Gaby in Brussels in 1939. My mom wears the fur coat I liked to borrow.

General Alexander von Falkenhausen, military commander for Belgium and Northern France. The general governed Belgium from the end of May 1940 until June 1944.
(Courtesy of the Centre de Recherches et D' Etudes Historiques de la Seconde Guerre Mondiale.)

German soldiers hoisting their flag in Brussels.
(Courtesy Musée Royale de L'Armée, Brussels.)

My class at the Lycee de Forest. I am sitting at the extreme left of the first row and Maria Van Weyenberg is standing at the extreme left in the back row. My beloved history teacher, Mademoiselle Denise Feytmans, sits in the middle of the front row.

Elizabeth Wolff, my best friend.

The German passport issued to
Suzanne Bamberger in November,
1940. Note the J and my new middle
name, Sara.

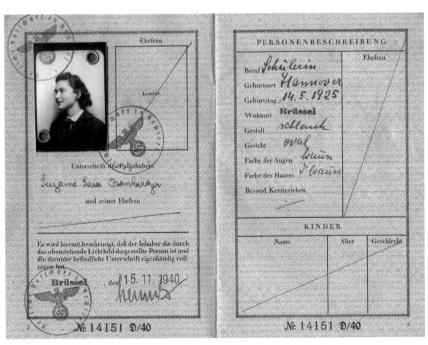

Suzanne Bamberger. 1941.

Sunbathing with Dèdè Hirschland in Brussels. 1941.

Nelly Altorfer and her baby
daughter, Lucette Wiame

Jean-Marie Wiame, my
absent-minded boss.
*(Courtesy of Professor
Jean-Marie Wiame.)*

Emile Altorfer, Nelly's brother and
a commander in the Armée Belges
des Partisans.
(Courtesy of Anne Altorfer.)

Emile, Annie, and
Mariette Altorfer.
*(Courtesy of Anne
Altorfer.)*

The Wiames lived
on the top floor of this
house. Note the balcony,
the site of my romantic
tête-a-tête with Emile.
*(Photo by David Loebl,
1991)*

At any time, citizens could expect to be searched by military patrols.
(Courtesy Musée Royale de L'Armée, Brussels.)

Tante Bets Vorwinden, the unquestionable boss of my second shelter.

This apartment house on the Avenue Louise became Brussels's Gestapo
headquarter. In its cellar, the newly arrested were often questioned
and tortured. To the great joy of the entire population, a British plane
machine-gunned the building in January 1944.
(Courtesy of the Centre de Recherches et D'Etudes Historiques
de la Seconde Guerre Mondiale.)

The governess
of the Grosfils
with her four
charges.

My bosses, Jacqueline and Jean Grosfils. *(Courtesy Jean-Pierre Grosfils.)*

Gina the chambermaid, my friend and coworker at the Grosfils'.

Madame Lebacqz and her dog, Toto, sitting on the stoop of her house on the Avenue de la Cascade in Brussels. My mother moved into the little furnished apartment in 1943. We continued to live there until we left for America in 1946.

My soldier cousin Ernest (Wertheimer) Worth, a member of the British Pioneer Corps, me, and Gaby. 1945.

The retreat of the German Army from Belgium was not very glorious. For days, the jubilant population lined the streets and celebrated silently.
(U.S. Army Signal Corps photo courtesy of Photothèque du Soir.)

Gaby with Gerald Bamberger
(right) and Rudy Bamberger
in front of our house at the
Avenue de la Cascade.

Marguerite Van Biema and "Mon General" Seligman after the war.

With my Red Cross unit waiting for the trains filled with the survivors of Hitler's work camps.

Gaby and my mom in front of a German tank abandoned during the Battle of the Bulge. Summer 1945.

Lucette and Jacques Wiame. 1945.

Assisting my father in his laboratory at the Chemo-Puro
Manufacturing Corporation in New York.

Hugo, Gaby,
Marguerite and
Suzanne Bamberger
in front of our house
in Forest Hills shortly
before my father's
death in December
1949.

Suzanne and Ernest Loebl's thirtieth wedding anniversary with Judy and David.

Chapter 7

The Endless War

Lucette, Nelly and Jean's infant daughter, was a very good baby. Nelly nursed her before she went to work and again when she returned in the late afternoon. The rest of the day, Lucette belonged to me. I was proud that Nelly entrusted her to my care. I enjoyed being a surrogate mother; there were other tasks I enjoyed less.

In the morning I cleaned. I hated it, and the house was never neat enough. Nelly sometimes threatened that she would send me to her aunt Titi so that I could be trained properly. I was better at my many other chores.

Midmorning Lucette, Pirou, and I went shopping, an arduous task. What vegetables did the store have that day? How long did I have to wait in line? Could I get potatoes, meat bones, carrots, cabbage? Had the sugar rations come in?

Back home I started to prepare dinner; it was always soup. I peeled potatoes, and the peels were cooked separately for Pirou. Nelly was very resourceful about augmenting our food supply. Some food was bought on the black market; other meals were prepared from what was available. We made our own sauerkraut—tons of it—from fresh cabbage. We pickled cucumbers, and then there were the herrings. For some unfathomable reason immense schools of herring passed near the Belgian coast; this became the country's chief source of protein. Recipes for cooking, smoking, steaming, or pickling these fish became an important topic of conversation. I used buckets to fetch the herring home from the market and spent hours cleaning them. It seemed there were always more. I remember the phone call Nelly received one evening after I had spent the better part of the day cleaning herring: "Yes," she said, "we would be happy to take another twenty pounds of herring!"

In spite of the herring and the black-market food, I was clearly not getting enough to eat. It was hard to tell, since I was fat. During the entire war, I was kidded a lot about being overweight in the face of extreme food shortages. I learned later that I actually suffered from hunger edema caused by the high-starch, low-protein wartime diet.

I rarely menstruated, and I developed a silver-dollar-sized sore on my leg that simply would not heal. I went to see Dr. Hertz, our physician, who continued to practice in his apartment. The Hertzes' daughter had married an Italian, now a high-ranking Fascist. Our good doctor's door sported a special seal issued by the Italian embassy protecting its residents from harassment and deportation. Hertz prescribed a salve, but the sore took nine months to heal.

Mademoiselle Feytmans had told us that Belgium has the highest rainfall in Europe. She was right. Winters were cold, clammy, and dark. There was not enough coal to heat the entire apartment and no running hot water. Even in peacetime my hands and feet were painfully cold in harsh weather. Now I developed frostbite.

By the winter of 1942, the aura of German invincibility had cracked. Hitler had pinned his hopes on winning the war in Russia before the snows came. Indeed, the Soviet army was in poor shape.

The German armies were also weak and exhausted, even though, during the preceding summer the world had witnessed a rebirth of the successful blitzkrieg. In southern Russia the German troops had overrun the Crimea and conquered the major ports of the Black Sea. The Germans had also hoped to conquer the Caucasus, from whose rich oil fields the Russian army obtained its fuel. Cutting the rail line linking Murmansk—the port through which the Allies supplied the Russian army and air force—and the interior was a high priority. Finally, Hitler was convinced that encircled Leningrad would surrender.

The Germans achieved none of their goals. Leningrad held fast for nine hundred days, though by the time the siege was lifted, one-third of the city's population of three million had died of hunger and related disease. Also, the Murmansk supply line also remained intact.

More important still was a seemingly minor battle involving the city of Stalingrad, located in southern Russia. It developed into a decisive turning point on the Eastern Front. The Germans almost overran Stalingrad in September 1942, but their troops were fatigued, and by November the Russians encircled the Germans. On January 31, 1943, the Germans around Stalingrad surrendered.

News from the Western Front also lifted our morale. On November 8, 1942, following a year of see-saw battles in Egypt and Libya, Allied troops— mostly American—commanded by General Dwight Eisenhower, landed at the other end of North Africa, in Morocco and Algeria. Encountering only Vichy French troops, whose resistance was half-hearted, the Allies advanced at a rapid pace. As a result of the invasion and the concurrent British breakthrough at El Alamein, in Egypt, the Germans and their Italian allies fell back on all fronts toward Tunisia. The Germans fought stubbornly through the winter, but they were finally defeated in the spring, and all the Axis troops in North Africa surrendered.

Addressing the world on the BBC in November 1942, Churchill said: "The [invasion of North Africa and El Alamein] must not be considered the end; it may possibly be the beginning of the end, but it certainly is the end of the beginning."

For those of us who were actually under the yoke of the Nazis, it did not matter much whether this was "the beginning of the end" or "the end of the beginning." Almost every day the Germans arrested someone we knew; others "disappeared." Time was not our friend.

Even without the radio, we knew that the war was coming closer. From 1941 on, the Royal Air Force bombed Germany and German-occupied territories. In Brussels the air was often filled with the comforting hum of Allied planes. The aim of these bombings was not only to bring the war home to Germany, but also to force the Germans to divert fighter planes from the Russian Front. Success of the air attacks was still limited. The German antiaircraft defenses were strong and massed along the coasts of northern France, Belgium, and Holland, the so-called Atlantic Wall. Underground agents in continental Europe helped the British to locate and eventually destroy many of these antiaircraft stations. According to Winston Churchill's memoirs, Belgian agents provided 80 percent of the information that enabled the RAF to evade and destroy the German air defense system.

Jean Wiame mounted a big map of Russia on the wall of the living room. We marked the zig-zagging front lines with colored pins. For the first time since the beginning of the war, there were victories to record. Each time the Germans suffered a setback in Russia, the Wiames bought some eggs and butter on the black market. Nelly baked a cake or, more often, a French fruit tart, and invited some friends to celebrate. These included Gert, the Anciaux, and even Professor Brachet, the Wiames' thesis adviser.

Conversation revolved around the war, politics, literature, food, and travel. I kept very quiet, enjoying the conversation. How I wished to be grown up and go on with my life!

Tension between the Belgian population and its oppressor mounted. The resistance executed an increasing number of Belgian Fascists and military personnel. The Germans retaliated by shooting more hostages—sometimes twenty at once! When particularly enraged, the authorities imposed strict curfews—from 9 P.M. to 6 A.M.—for the entire population, ordered the closure of movie houses and theaters, canceled sporting events, and requisitioned thousands of bicycles without compensation.

Once a week I had a day off. I usually went to see my mother. She had traded her room at Dominick and Delphine's house for a small apartment in Etterbeck. Even though the apartment was shabby and makeshift, I loved coming home. For a few hours, I did not have to be on my best behavior and could shed my make-believe personality. My mom and I laughed a lot, and she sometimes had some extra food for me. I often left restored.

The visits, however, were not always peaceful. My mother kept urging me to be good, stay home, and lie low. "War," she would always say, "is not for fun." But I did not want to be good and asked her why on earth I should be reasonable.

"If I have no fun," I said, "the Nazis at the very least managed to poison years of my life."

Fortunately for my ultimate survival, I could never figure out how to be bad. I also was much concerned with the safety of my protectors and behaved as unobtrusively as possible, looking like the perfect mother's helper.

Since I was not in a camp, lived in relative comfort, and even freely roamed the streets, I realized that I was comparatively well off. Still I was often angry and ill at ease.

I liked and admired my hosts, but I was intimidated by their virtue and generosity. They risked their freedom and lives to save mine. I hated being such a burden. Why was I such an outcast? I had never harmed anyone!

Having to be grateful is hard to cope with, especially if it is for something as fundamental as saving one's own life, so I tried to minimize the danger we all faced. In some ways this was easy, because to a certain extent life was drearily mundane. It was precisely the juxtaposition of the daily dullness with the horror of the Holocaust that was characteristic of the crazy times I was living in.

My limited social life also included visits to the Salomons. Their lives in their little illegal apartment were not all that different from those they had led before the war. Gretel Salomon still managed to put a tasty meal on the table, which she served punctually at 12:30. Martin lived with his parents, and neither he nor his mother ever left the apartment. Harry, who prided himself on his flawless, unaccented French and his sophisticated look, did all the shopping. My visits were welcome distractions. I enjoyed seeing Martin blush during our very innocent conversations or whenever I touched him accidentally.

I also enjoyed visits to the Hirschlands. Gertt, Pitt, and Dédé did not live with their parents, and wartime etiquette prevented me from asking where they were, but Alma Hirschland listened to me patiently. Their economically vital scrap metal business had been declared a Jewish enterprise years earlier and had a German manager. Yet even now Pappy Hirschland arrived every morning. When a client showed up, Pappy introduced himself as "Hirschland" in his deep voice. At the end of the day, he walked the twenty minutes that separated his factory from his hiding place. During that walk he changed his identity from Hirschland to Albert Van Eik, his false name.

The Hirschlands were always ready to help others. On more than one occasion Pappy told my mother not to worry about money. As usual he put it so that it seemed we were doing him a favor. "Mrs. Bamberger," he would say, "it might be good for us to have some money in America. So just let me know if you need some cash."

The Hirschlands had adopted Roli, my former rival. Like all of us, Roli's family had received their deportation orders during the summer of 1942. The family had moved to a hotel on the outskirts of town. Within a week their hiding place had been denounced, and the Gestapo picked up Roli's parents and brother. Roli fortunately was out on a date with Gert. The Nazis awaited her return, but, forewarned by a neighbor, she avoided the trap. She went to the Hirschlands, who treated her like a daughter, buying her excellent false papers and finding her a safe place to stay.

Like during the previous two years, we spent New Year's Eve with the Salomons. Harry unearthed a bottle of wine, Gretel cooked a decent meal, and we welcomed in 1943. The broadcast of the BBC was as upbeat as usual. We laughed at a currently circulating joke about someone listening to the BBC five years hence. "What did they say?" a friend asked. "They are coming soon."

I looked at the Salomons and my mother. I was much too old to be celebrating New Year's Eve with them. I should be out dancing. If I survive, I promised myself, I'll always party on New Year's Eve.

Unable to begin living my fantasy, I returned to the Wiames. Nelly and I had become friends, and I was happier there than I had been before Lucette was born. I was less rebellious and truly admired the way Nelly combined family life and career. She liked the way I handled the baby, and she must have resigned herself to the constant state of disarray in the house.

I had so much work that my day passed quickly. As before there often was intellectually stimulating company in the evenings, and I kept hoping that Emile would show up. My books comforted me, if he did not.

Because he was working full-time for the resistance, Emile lived separately from his wife and daughter. Once in a while Mariette met Emile at the Wiames' home. Sometimes Mariette stayed overnight, sometimes she came with four-year-old Annie, and sometimes, to my chagrin, the Wiames vacated their house so that Mariette and Emile would have undisturbed time together. Then I too left, spending a weekend with my mother or the Vorwindens.

Mariette awed me. She was the same age as Nelly, and they had been classmates at the Ecole Normale, the French equivalent of a teacher's college. That's how Mariette had met Emile. In 1937, five years earlier, Mariette and Emile had been delegated by the Free University of Brussels to assist the Loyalists (anti-Fascists) during Spain's ill-fated civil war. After their return, they secretly joined the Communist Party. Now I gathered that Mariette, like Emile, worked for the resistance, but these things were not discussed.

Emile had retained his Swiss citizenship, which afforded his family a certain protection. Nevertheless, since both he and Mariette worked for the underground and were at risk of being arrested, they decided to send Annie to stay with relatives in Switzerland.

Annie was to leave the following week, and this was her farewell visit with her father, aunt, and uncle. Loving little children, I volunteered to feed her. Mariette accepted gladly—Annie was a fussy eater and mealtimes were tedious. As I tried to convince Annie to eat, I studied her serious little face. With its dark eyes and dimpled chin, it was a miniature replica of her father's. She was about to be separated from all those she knew and loved! Would she ever be able to understand and forgive her parents for risking their lives to save the world from plunging back into the Dark Ages?

Chapter 8
The Diary

At the end of May 1943, I spent a weekend at the Vorwindens'. As usual I was lovesick and lonely. I took an old notebook and scribbled a love letter to Emile. Venting my feelings, even if only on paper, offered relief. I haphazardly started keeping a diary. Initially, many of the entries are letters, most addressed to Emile, but I also chatted with Pitt and Elizabeth. As time went on, the entries simply recorded the events of the day. The diary gives little information about the actual events that took place at the time.

To prevent identification should the diary fall into German hands, I made some efforts to disguise names. I recorded some of the information in the shorthand that I had so laboriously learned at the Institut Meysman. At the time, I predicted that I would not be able to decipher this stenography later. Time has proven me partially correct. I kept my diary, sporadically, until December 1944. Then I no longer needed, or had time for, solitary introspection.

For a variety of reasons, I have ignored my diary since I wrote it decades years ago. Rereading it now, I believe it to be an accurate reflection of a most unusual time. I enjoy meeting the teenager who grew up under such difficult circumstances. I like her guts, although I rather mind her sentimentality and her flowery, cliché-ridden style. I am shocked that she did not appreciate the seriousness of her situation; I am horrified at the chances she took, touched by her loneliness, surprised by her innocence, grieved by her losses, bored by her repetitiveness, and, above all, glad that she managed to survive to tell her story.

From here on I intersperse the diary entries with the recollections of my life in Belgium. The original diary is in French. I translated it as faithfully as possible, deleting material that now is meaningless and clarifying, when possible, obscure passages.

5/26/43

Emile, Chèri,

I found the love letters [hidden in a linen closet] that you wrote to Mariette before you were married. I know that I should not have read them, but I did and turned extremely jealous. I too love you. Why, I wonder?

Love is like a dream. Once you wake up it vanishes and the beloved, once again, is a common mortal.

For now, however, you are real. I worship you. I love your cynicism, your smile, your mouth, your warm hands, your voice. I wish I was like you. I tremble whenever the Germans report a mass arrest.

I know that there is no point to this love, but I would like to be a small part of your life. Perhaps I could work with you.

When I met you, my life had been turned upside-down. I was homesick. I hated being a maid. I hated being grateful. I hated being told what to do. I hated growing up that fast.

Then you came. You smiled and joked and I made peace with myself. I discovered that one can be both a member of the proletariat and an intellectual. At long last I identify with the Communists and am a proud member of the working class. Our ideals may not come true in our lifetime, but Communism is humankind's natural destiny.

I am writing this—my first love letter—sitting on the balcony of my bedroom at the Vorwindens'. The little terrace is right under the roof. I have a wonderful view. The Forêt de Soignes [the large forest abutting Brussels to the south] fills the horizon. I see the spire of the Altitude Cent in Forest, where I used to live. To

the right are the towers of the university. Will I ever be able to
go there?

I look in the direction of Nelly's house. Perhaps Mariette is
there waiting for you. Perhaps you will sleep there tonight?

Last winter, you usually stayed with us twice a week. You
showed up unannounced. But somehow I always knew when you
would come and cleaned up my room, "just in case."

Time to go to bed. I kiss you very hard.

It so happened that on May 27, 1943, the day after I wrote this letter,
Mariette Altorfer was arrested by the Gestapo as she boarded the streetcar
to go to work. She was first interrogated at Gestapo headquarters on the
Avenue de Louise, then she was transferred to Saint Gilles, the local prison.

Rumor had it that Mariette's cellmate was a stool pigeon. Unsuspectingly,
Mariette might have told this double agent about les Partisans Armés—the
restistance group she and Emile worked for—or that her in-laws sheltered a
Jewish girl. For the Wiames safety, as well as for my own, I could no longer
stay with them.

I fortunately could return to the Vorwindens until I found another
hiding place. Here is my next diary entry, written two days after Mariette's
arrest. Emile tried very hard to have his wife released. After a few weeks in
prison, Mariette was deported "east," destination unknown.

5/29/43

Chèri,

You must be beside yourself with concern and grief. Even
though disaster is always around the corner, one is unprepared
when it actually arrives. For me Mariette's arrest was a total
surprise.

This morning, I wanted to hear your voice, and phoned [Nelly's
house] under some pretext or other. When there was no answer,
I worried. I told myself to forget about it. Unfortunately my
foreboding was correct.

I still don't know exactly what happened to Mariette, and part
of me still refuses to believe that anything did go wrong.

Nelly and you are made of sterner stuff than most people.
I can't imagine either of you ever crying.

Nelly told me that she felt it would be unsafe for me to continue staying with them. After "giving me the sack," Nelly added a lecture.

As usual, she started out by saying that it was for my own good. Nelly claims that I am too sure of myself. Perhaps I do come across too strongly. Yet, I know how difficult it is for me to ask for something for myself.

I am unhappy about leaving the Wiames. I'll miss Lucette and Pirou. There will be no more chance encounters with you. Will you still remember me? I suppose that in time I too could forget you, but for as long as I live, your memory will remain bright and shining.

I want to join the resistance, but have no idea of how to go about it. Perhaps then I can work with you.

Every night the Belgian radio broadcast from London signed off with: *"On les aura les Boches"* (We'll get the Huns.) This indeed had become the battle cry of the entire Belgian middle class. By the spring of 1943, resistance to the Germans had become a mass movement. On May 10, for instance, the third anniversary of the war, people protested by not going to work. On national holidays everyone went to Sainte Gudule to attend mass.

It was not easy, and the anxiety level of the entire population reached new highs. The Belgian Fascist Party was still extremely active. Its head, Leon Degrelle, wore a German uniform and headed a battalion that fought alongside the Germans on the Soviet front. It was rumored that Himmler visited von Falkenhausen in Brussels and demanded that the Germans become tougher.

Organized resistance was becoming increasingly effective, gradually crippling Belgium's transportation system. Government services were infiltrated. Some postal employees read letters that informers sent to the Gestapo, and warned those about to be arrested before dispatching the mail any further.

The loss of my hiding place at the Wiames' trapped poor Tante Bets. She felt obliged to shelter me until I found another refuge. It was understandable that she did not want me to stay with them for very long. She feared that my presence would bring the Germans to her house and blow her own flimsy cover. She also felt that my rather liberated attitude was a bad influence on her own very subdued, obedient children. Tension between me and Tante Bets mounted, as did my boredom.

Almost immediately I started searching for a family that, in exchange for household help or child care, would give me room and board. Such "au pair" jobs were an excellent cover. People, in general, pay little attention to domestics, especially in fancy neighborhoods. It was also quite natural for a young girl to look after children.

I fortunately continued to have food stamps. These were delivered to us every month by the De Backers, our benefactors, to whom I owed my refuge with the Wiames. Every month Mr. De Backer, a former functionary, picked up our stamps at the town hall of our last legal residence. Taking advantage of the perpetual bureaucratic confusion, the Belgian authorites continued issuing food stamps to many illegals throughout the war, thus making a major contribution to their survival.

Because household help was in short supply, I hoped to find another hiding place rapidly. I had to select my prospective employer with great care. I often followed up leads supplied by friends. I also knew of a curious "employment agency" whose main function seemed to be finding safe havens for those hunted by the Germans. Most of the pertinent information was not expressed in words.

I went to the office of this employment agency, explaining that I needed a job, barely hinting at the fact that I was Jewish. The women behind the desk understood and gave me the name and address of a prospective employer. The agency had not actually talked to their client about hiring someone hiding from the Germans. I assumed that they had made reasonably sure that they sent me to people trustworthy enough not to denounce me to the Gestapo.

When I went to the actual interview, I had to decide in a flash whether I could dare reveal my secret. If not, I could refuse the job or make a poor impression. If I felt that I could take a chance, I hesitatingly told my story—sometimes admitting that I was Jewish, sometimes explaining that I had to leave home because otherwise I would be conscripted and sent to a forced-labor camp in Germany. In either case, I would assure my prospective employer that, if need be, I would swear that they were ignorant of my illegal status. My search for a new shelter took much longer than I had expected.

◆

A few days after Mariette's arrest, I learned that Pitt Hirschland had been caught as he and a non-Jewish friend attempted to cross into Switzerland. The Swiss border guard turned the two young men over to the Germans. Pitt and his friend were apparently shipped to Germany by train, but details were uncertain. Eventually, Pitt managed to write to his parents from Oranienburg, a forced-labor camp near Berlin. Mr. and Mrs. Hirschland never told me that they knew Pitt to be relatively safe and that they even managed to send him food parcels. To me Pitt's fate remained a mystery.

6/3/43

Pitt, I just heard that you "disappeared." Where are you? Why don't you write? I admire you for having the guts to try to get out of this hellhole. Your family thinks otherwise.

This war makes us grow up very fast, but our parents keep clinging. Don't they realize that children, like birds, must leave the nest? Your mother is very strong and, as always, very supportive. I hope that you too are strong and clever.

I desperately want to do something except save my skin. Yesterday I saw René Fuss and asked him to help me join the resistance. He said that he would try. I also approached Suzy, my milliner friend, but she sent me packing. My mother would have a fit if she knew what I was trying to do. If only this cursed war were over!

Given my passion for Emile, it must seem strange that I think of you often. I escape reality by daydreaming and I often fantasize about you loving me.

I have turned prettier—at least people often tell me that I am attractive. I can also tell from the way people look at me. I would enjoy showing you this "new me," like I used to show you my new clothes.

In La Panne I fell in love with Gert. Later, when he started going with Roli, I realized what a fool I had made of myself. I worried about who knew. Your mother? My mother? Gert? Roli? I was mortified and resolved that I never again would love anyone without being loved back. Since you obviously were not interested in love, I turned you into my best friend—a friend with whom I could talk about everything: music, theater, books, clothes, fashion, torn stockings . . .

I wish I could revive these happy memories tonight . . . but it hurts too much.

♦

6/4/43

Pitt, since I learned of your arrest, I keep thinking about you. I hope that they will not find out that you are a Jew.

I went to the movies tonight with Suzy and Willy, her fiancé. My mother would have a fit if she knew.

The newsreel was very funny. They started out with a battle scene: shooting, explosions, noise, flashes. Then there was total darkness. Since the Germans were losing the battle, there was no actual war news. No reference even to an organized "regrouping in previously chosen, consolidated positions."

The Germans no longer infuriate me as they did in the past. The soldiers actually make me sad. I can't believe that the whole world is full of men willing to serve as cannon fodder.

The sky is filled with airplanes. Where are they headed for tonight? Time to go to sleep, I am tired.

By the summer of 1943 we not only heard the planes, but the ground was often littered with strips of tin foil. The volume and frequency of the Allied sorties made it obvious that air superiority had shifted to the Allies, the German antiaircraft defenses, now equipped with radar, were so efficient, however, that Allied aircraft losses were high. Britain's clever air-defense expert correctly speculated that a radar beam could be fooled by a simple strip of tin foil. The clouds of tin foil released by the bombers enabled the planes to reach their targets. All the major German cities were hit: Hamburg, Essen, Cologne, and even Berlin. For us in Brussels, the glittering strips of foil were tangible proof that help was on the way.

I am depressed and discouraged. I can't remember when I last felt that sad. For once I regret that my parents emigrated to Belgium.

I have no youth, no boyfriends. I can't play or even participate in sports. There is not even school. I never meet anyone my own age. Why? Because of a band of hoodlums! When will they cease to exist?

I hope that my children will not have to suffer like me.

◆

I have not yet gotten to the point of rejoicing when the Allies bomb German civilians, but I am no longer against the bombings. It is "them" or "us," and if I am to perish, I want it to be "them" and "us."

Until now most of those who were deported were strangers; that was ghastly enough. But now the brutes are touching my friends, and my rage is unremitting. Pitt, I remember when we went to concerts together. I was so happy and proud you asked me out.

◆

I live among strangers who do not understand me. They could not, even if they tried. What I write here does not make much sense, but my diary is my friend, and writing makes me feel good.

◆

6/6/43

Pitt, my thoughts are constantly with you. Downstairs Lientje [Vorwinden] plays the piano. I miss music. Perhaps one day soon I'll go to a concert.

Anyone reading my diary must think that I am boy-crazy, falling in love with anyone wearing pants. Not so, but I cannot survive on hate alone. My heart overflows with love, but does not know whom to love or what cause to espouse.

If only I had a friend, somebody to talk to, somebody who belongs to me alone. How strange that right now, when I would perish without friends, I am so utterly alone. How much I changed during the last year! How hard it is to carry all these burdens by myself.

Sometimes I wonder what the history books of the future will be like. How will the author retell the current events? Will the students analyze World War II as we studied the Napoleonic wars? There will be discussion of the battles, the food shortages, the concentration camps. Nobody will remember the colossal suffering of the ordinary bystanders.

When I was a small child, I believed God protected each of us. Now I know that He cares as much about each of us as we care about ants we squash with our feet. Yesterday I took a bus. I knew that the countryside through which it passed was lovely. But the trip was like life: The windows of the bus were misted, and I could not see a thing.

♦

6/8/43

It seems unreal. In spite of my heartache, I cheered up. I pretend that I don't understand why my world feels less doomed. Perhaps, like an ostrich, I manage to ignore reality. I daydream and live happily in my unreal world. Deep down I may still be depressed, but I simply don't want to know.

I visited my mother yesterday. She spoke to Mr. Salomon, who in turn spoke to Tante Bets. I sense trouble.

Airplanes are flying overhead . . . I wish the war were over.

At the Vorwindens I occupied myself during the long day as best I could. I had gone to see Mademoiselle Goulart, the secretary of the Lycée de Forest. My former school was trying to help Jewish students keep up with their classwork and was supplying textbooks and assignments. I struggled ineffectively with high-school geometry. I was better at making my way through a detailed history of the Etruscans that I had borrowed from the Wiames. Mostly, however, I read endless back issues of *Marie Claire*, a woman's magazine, that Tante Bets had assembled in the basement. I became addicted to stories on "How to Catch a Man," "How to Evaluate a New Date," "How to Become Glamorous in 30 Minutes After a Full Day in the Office," and "How to Save a Marriage." These stories fed my ever-growing fantasy life and made me forget for a short while my precarious situation.

I knew that I was giving Tante Bets a hard time. I was a free agent, coming and going as I pleased, and this alone might have worried her. Being very young, I felt myself invulnerable and secure. I went downtown needlessly, although the city was patrolled by turncoat Jews who helped the Gestapo identify and arrest illegals. On one of my expeditions downtown, a short man who kept looking me straight in the eyes, barred my way. Was he the famous Jacques? I tried to pass, but he continued to hinder my progress by stepping to the same side I did. Finally he let me go. My knees were shaking, and I resolved to stay at home more, and probably did for several days or weeks.

I was aimless and restless. Life was completely schizophrenic. I had a false name and bright red hair. My immediate aim—finding household employment—was at total odds with my long-term goals. Yet the present was so real that I could not fathom that household employment was only a temporary measure.

Now that I had no job, I spent more time at my mother's apartment located near the National Rifle Range. In peacetime the Tir National was used for military maneuvers and to teach the Belgian soldiers sharpshooting. The Germans used it to execute prisoners and ever-increasing numbers of hostages.

At dawn when my mother and I were awakened by the noise of machine-gun fire, we knew that the war had claimed additional innocent victims. We were aggrieved and nauseated by our powerlessness. All told, during the occupation, more than a thousand people were executed at the Tir National.

My mother was very distrustful of her current landlord, a former police officer, who she felt might be tempted to turn her in and collect a reward. I did not know whether her instinct was correct or if she was just being overly cautious. In any case, she too looked for new quarters.

6/10/43

The weather is lovely. After days of rain the sun is shining.
I am all by myself. The Vorwindens have gone out. I am sitting
in the gazebo. The garden borders a wheat field. The wind rustles
the sheaves and makes them sing. The cherry tree is full of ripe,
tempting fruit—which I may not touch.

If one closes one's ears one could almost believe the world is
at peace. But the sky is full of humming planes.

I just did like Eve—I ate cherries off the "forbidden tree." The
chance I took, however, was smaller than hers. I do not live in
paradise.

I am "good" today. I stayed home even though I could have gone to the movies. I have no regrets.

Yesterday I went to see René Fuss. He arranged for me an interview with a woman who needed a mother's helper for her six children. They live in Keerbergen, a small village outside Brussels.

Emile, you would not have been proud of me. During the interview the woman said that I acted like a young bourgeois girl and probably could not do all the necessary work. She might be right; in any case, I would hate living there. But then, Communism does not necessarily aim to lower the living standards of the middle class to those of the proletariat, but to raise the lifestyle of all concerned. Whatever, I hope the woman does not want me and that I find another job.

Jean and Nelly are really looking after me and are trying to find me a place. I am touched, I would never have thought so. I guess there are people who simply "do" and don't talk about it. Their friends Robert and Didine may have a job for me near Liège.

◆

6/12/43

I did not get the job in Liège. Fortunately, the one in Keerbergen also fell through. Why, I wonder, did I want to move to Liège so badly?

Perhaps to escape close supervision. My mother does not realize how fettered I am here in Brussels. If by chance she understood, she would be very sad.

I want to have a boyfriend. I terribly miss not having one. I am jealous each time I see a boy and a girl holding hands. I am lonely. I know nobody my own age. I am eighteen and should "live." Instead I simply "exist."

"Be careful," say my mother and her friends. It is easy for them to talk that way. They had their lives. I can't understand how Martin and the others listen. They are stupid. Our life belongs to us. We can risk it if we choose. Why did I imagine Liège would be so great?

>   Liège, the city that sings
>   Liège, on the banks of the Meuse
>   Liège, a small university town

Perhaps in Liège I would have had some time for myself. I even might have been able to join a tennis club.

Now I cry. Life is idiotic. Why bother.

♦

Twilight. The last light glows in the dark. I sit on my balcony. The view is breathtaking. My cherry tree is there. Without sun it is still beautiful, but somber. I would love to paint it.

The world is so beautiful and rich. Why and for what are people killing each other?

Pitt, today for the first time I realized that you might never come back, that even now you might be dead. When the sun shines again, will you be missing? I thought of your possible death for a split second only, then I pushed it out of my mind.

♦

I wish I could forget everything, if only for a few hours. I miss listening to music.

Night is falling. Night life is another wartime casualty. The last streetcar rumbles to the depot. The city too sleeps. It is completely dark.

♦

6/14/43

Maman,

Just now I would like to be with you. I almost went to see you. What a pity that you are not here right now. I found a little secret garden a few minutes from the Vorwindens' house. It is a small, wooded glade in a forgotten corner of the Park de Woluvé. Grass carpets the entire floor of my little room; shrubs and trees enclose it. I am all alone, except for right now while a man passes by. Now he is gone.

There is a light breeze. The leaves rustle, it reminds me of the ocean, of vacations. I am reading a book about the Spanish Civil war: "Salud Camarada." Some passages make me feel good and I read them over and over.

For example:

"To die in bed . . . what a horrible prospect!"

"To dedicate oneself to a cause . . . how essential."

Gaby came to see me earlier today. I enjoyed her visit
very much.

My sister was still hidden at the Vinckes' in Baasrode, one hour by bus
from Brussels. I did not see her very often. The Vinckes were extremely
devout, and they sheltered Gaby because the Catholic church had decreed
that it would try "at least to save the [Jewish] children."

The Vinckes also needed the stipend my mother paid for Gaby's care.
Romanie Vincke, who after the arrest of her husband was the head of the
family, had hoped that my sister would convert to Catholicism and broached
the subject—but once only. Gaby refused because, young as she was, she felt
that she "could not abandon her own religion, since her people were going
through such hard times."

Since thirteen-year-old Gaby could not go to school, she spent most of
her day in the barn reading pornographic books the Vinckes stored for
some aristocratic friends. Romanie, doubtlessly aware of the nature of the
books, asked the parish priest whether Gaby could read them. The priest,
who knew that Gaby's was a "heathen," gave his permission. The local teacher
and the village doctor also knew that Gaby was Jewish, but nobody alerted
the local authorities.

All the Vinckes grew very fond of my sister. Since his arrest as a member
of the resistance, there had been no news from Joseph, nor did they ever
figure out who had betrayed him. Romanie supported her parents-in-law
and three young children on her small teacher's salary. In winter it was
damp and freezing cold, and aside from mounds of potatoes flavored with
bacon there was little food.

6/15/43

It is mid-June, but the weather is still cold and miserable.
I can't understand people like the Vorwindens. Their life has no
purpose even though they could have done with it whatever they
wanted.

Tante Bets's and Oom Heim's attitude is so different from the
one we had at home. Take school, for example. Neither my mom
nor I ever took it very seriously. If one worries too much about
grades, one does not learn anything else.

To me it seems peculiar that fifteen-year-old Lientje cannot wash a dish. Tante Bets and Oom Hein had a lot of formal education, speak four languages, play the piano, and are good at sports, games, and cards. They traveled far and wide. And yet, today they behave rather badly, much worse than uneducted Bertha, or my mother's Delphine.

Chapter 9

Of Love and Loss

Throughout my entire stay at the Vorwindens', I continued to visit the Wiames. I had the keys and went during the day to borrow books. Once as I entered the apartment, I met a twenty-five-year-old man. I was terrified, but not nearly as much as Boris, the escaped Soviet prisoner of war the Wiames were sheltering. After both of us recovered, he was pleased to see me. We had no common language, but Boris managed to suggest that we have some fun. I was getting to be an expert at extricating myself from such propositions. I selected a few books and stayed away for a while.

Sometimes I visited the Wiames in the evening and chatted. Once in a while, I babysat for Lucette. One such evening Emile came, unannounced as always. The air was mild, and we sat on the small balcony overhanging the brook in which I used to catch worms for Nelly's axolotl. Juliette's balcony in Verona could not have been more romantic. Emile puffed on his pipe, his thin lips twisted in an enigmatic smile, and said very little. There was no need to speak; my own inflamed heart provided all I needed. I explained that I was fed up being both a spectator and a victim in this war. I asked Emile if he could find me a job in the resistance. He promised that he would try.

I now understand why Emile Altorfer was reluctant to help me join the resistance. I was already hiding, I looked Jewish, and I had questionable false papers and a slight German accent. These were poor qualifications for a courier, the job most often assigned to women. It was much safer that I continue living underground as inconspicuously as possible. Emile and Rene Fuss, whom I had also approached with my request, never said so outright, but in retrospect I believe that their assessment of the situation was correct. At the time, however, I did not accept it. Until the end of the occupation, I hoped to take a more active part in fighting the Germans.

I felt that my stay with the Vorwindens was depleting our savings. We paid Tante Bets fifty francs a day for my keep. The sum, about fifteen U.S. dollars, was certainly not excessive, but I feared that it strained our finances. We had a limited amount of money, and I worried whether it would last us through the war. "It is bad enough to be illegal Jews," I kept telling my mother. "It would be still worse if we were penniless." Our fixed expenses included fifty francs a day for Gaby's board at the Vinckes', rent for my mother's apartment, her food (some of which was bought on the black market), and a small amount of pocket money for me. We also needed money for new sets of false papers when the old ones became too common and would be easily spotted if scrutinized. I felt strongly that we needed to have cash reserves for bribes or to possibly finance a costly escape to Switzerland.

The atmosphere at the Vorwindens' had become openly hostile. In addition to being annoyed at my many real and imagined misdeeds and the increased danger to her family, Tante Bets believed that I was promiscuous and disobedient.

6/20/43

I have not written in my diary for a while. Wednesday I went to the movie with Lien. As an excuse for going downtown, we told Tante Bets that I needed to make a long-distance phone call to Malines. This call had to be made from the railroad station. We saw "Viennese Blood," a frothy German film. I enjoyed it.

After the movie I went to stay with my mother, who was most happy to see me. Once there I started crying, I simply could not stop.

On Friday morning mother and I went to Beersel [my mother's favorite excursion]. The weather was perfect, the countryside magnificent—everything was peaceful. We did not meet a soul during the entire walk.

When I returned to the Vorwindens', I discovered that silly Lien had confessed the movie escapade to her mother. This was the straw that broke the camel's back. Tante Bets asked Mr. Salomon to ask my mother to come and see her.

That evening I wrote Tante Bets a letter of apology, and made myself cry [with the help of one of the many onions stored in the attic next to my room] when I gave it to her.

After that I went over to visit with Jean and Nelly. Lucette was awake. She is becoming a real cute little girl.

Old Mrs. Altorfer and Caroline, her helper, were visiting. It seems as if Mrs. Altorfer's hair turned whiter since Mariette's arrest. Caroline was told that I am Jewish and she looked at me with curiosity.

I went to the Salomons' and had one of Gretel's fabulous dinners. René Fuss dropped in to say hello. He is optimistic about the way the war goes. I hope that he is right.

◆

6/24/43

Good grief! My mother came to listen to Tante Bets's complaining about me. They really took me to pieces. After they were through talking, there was nothing good left about me. The most ridiculous thing, however, was that Tante Bets informed my mother that I go out in the middle of the night to meet up with strange men. I wonder whether my mother made that one up? This bit of news is both funny and unpleasant. What does Tante Bets or my mother mean?

When Tante Bets told my mother that I went out at night "to meet up with strange men," my poor mother, who really had plenty of other worries, believed her. She attributed my downfall to "the sex hormones that coursed through my blood" and to the fact that I "grew up without a father."

Since I was still only dreaming of being kissed by a boy, I was completely mystified by these accusations. I finally managed to calm my mother. Only years later did I realize that Tante Bets had discovered my diary and took the innocent fantasies it recorded as facts.

◆

Unfortunately I can no longer confide in my mother. The less she knows, the better it is. She is a terrible gossip and her conclusions are always wrong. Emile, I often think about you. Will I ever see you again?

◆

6/25/43

Life is a piece of shit. I do not feel that I belong anywhere, and I usually feel ill at ease. Is it the war or am I setting up these unbridgeable gaps? I felt completely at home when I was living with the Wiames. Yet now I do not think that I could ask them for a sandwich if I were hungry.

I went over to their house today, visited, did the dishes, and read. I do not think that Emile still spends nights there.

One day as I traveled around Brussels, I suddenly ran into Elizabeth Wolff. We were so surprised to meet each other that we barely talked and decided to write each other instead. Since we did not wish to exchange addresses, we decided to use Suzy Tamineau's milliner's shop as a letter drop. When asked, Suzy agreed. I wrote Elizabeth a letter and a few weeks later I had an answer. Here is the only letter I received from Elizabeth during the entire two years we lived underground.

Received on 6/26/43:

My Little Friend,

We have not met for a long time, but I see you in front of me as if the last time was yesterday and we just had one of our endless, acrimonious discussions. I was so happy to hear from you. I am sorry that you had to move. I hope that everything will turn out for the best.

It would be difficult to meet. I never know when I am coming to Brussels. Today, when you'll read this letter it will be another day, my trip again was unexpected. The milliner is very nice. How lucky we are to have her. This way we are at least able to write to each other.

I would love to see you. We now are separated from one another for almost ten months. I do not know how, and with whom you live, but I do not see anybody young, unless you include children aged from zero to two years. I am becoming totally dumb and uneducated. I have not studied for a long time; I simply cannot concentrate. I don't do anything, and yet I am terribly busy.

Just now I am happy. Listen: Our neighbors, who do not know our real situation, are very good to us. Their family consists of a 42-year-old father, his 22-year-old daughter, her 23-year-old husband, and their children: a 22-month-old girl and a two-week-old baby.

During the last nine months, obviously, when the young mother was pregnant, I sometimes took care of the little girl. I wheeled her around in her stroller and taught her various things. Two weeks ago, when her mother went to the hospital to have a big, fat baby boy, the little girl moved in with us. She eats and sleeps here. That is my happiness. It will end tomorrow since then my little friend returns to her own house.

I'll suppose that I will continue to take care of her, since her mother cannot manage with the two little ones. The little boy sleeps in the crib I made. Sometimes I am allowed to feed him a bottle. Then I am in seventh heaven. It is the only pleasure that I have for the moment.

When did you visit the mother of Annette? [This refers to our zoology teacher at the Lycée de Forest.] I do not congratulate you on your spelling; it is as atrocious as ever. I cannot verify your other, reported progress [my telling her that I now was an enthusiastic Marxist.] For that we need to have a couple of stormy discussions. Courage. The time will come. Merde [Shit]. My handwriting is bad, but I am writing fast, so I can tell you a lot.

My little friend, tell your mother, to whom I send my best regards, not to try to cross the Swiss border.

If I were in school, I would now be ready to enter the Rhetorique [the last grade of the lyceé]. If this war lasts I'll lose two years of school. Soon I'll turn 17! Ha, our "golden youth"! I wonder what will come next.

You remember the little René, Eva's nephew? He is "far away." [He and his parents were arrested and deported.] Don't tell anybody, because even his grandparents don't know. My parents? There is a rumor that they may be in Theresienstadt [the Nazis' model camp]. But, who knows? Perhaps they are already in Poland, and that is hell. Isn't life beautiful?

Well, what will be, will be. I have become incapable of making projects or of having fantasies. I, who loved to daydream! But nobody knows who will be left after all this is over.

The baby is sleeping in my room. The light disturbs her. She thinks it is morning. I am turning off the light, otherwise she'll cry.

A big hug. Courage.
Your Sparrow

◆

6/27/43

Yesterday I received my first letter from Elizabeth, my little sparrow. I am happy and grateful for the letter. Poor Elizabeth sounds so very sad.

Suzy T's fiance, Willy, must report to a forced-labor camp. It is of course none of my business, but I will try to convince him not to go.

Pitt, I went to see your mother. She is brave, concerned about others, and sweet as always. I sense, however, that she worries a lot about you. It is now three months since you vanished. I despair of your safety. I hope that you are still with your non-Jewish friend.

Today I received a sexual proposition. My suitor is Jerome, Bertha's 52-year-old husband!

◆

Tante Bets always insists that I am not to buy her any presents. Well, today I found a box of raspberries, at the official price, which I bought for my mother. The good tante made such a fuss about the raspberries and my obligation to the Vorwindens that I ended up giving them to her.

My stay at the Vorwindens dragged on. I still went to the Wiames as often as possible, flirting and having myself teased by Jean and Gert Ochinsky. I was still sensitive about being overweight, which prompted people to needle me about having too much to eat while others starved.

♦

Tonight I phoned Jean Wiame. Gert was there. They wanted to know whether I had lost weight. I said that I did. They told me to send them a photo of myself or come over so they could see for themselves. I said I would be right over.

I had of course not lost any weight, but as always enjoyed my visit. I did not stay very long, because of the business of "meeting up with strangers in the middle of the night."

It is already 1 A.M. now. I went to bed two hours ago. I am unable to fall asleep. I am hungry.

Food available with stamps was way less than what I required. I was often so hungry that I sneaked into the Vorwindens' kitchen and stole some raw oats and sugar. I particularly relished the sugar. I could not understand how, in peacetime, I had overlooked this delicacy and promised myself to eat plenty of plain sugar if I survived this calamity.

Throughout the occupation, food was freely available in many upscale stores and even restaurants. My mother had discovered a pastry shop that served hot-fudge sundaes. She gave me the required sum of money and one day I went to the shop and ordered my treat. Reasonably enough, the clerk asked to be paid before she served me the ice cream. This lack of trust offended me. My ice-cream sundae was delicious, but all I remembered was being alone in this fancy tearoom. I ate my dessert with a profound sense of sadness.

7/6/43

Today I am all by myself in the big house. I love that. I love living alone. The only object I miss at present is a radio. I would like to listen to music I pick. Gaby came to see me and it cheered me up.

I am torn. Whom do I love more: my mother or Emile? Or, to put it differently, what is my duty?

On the one hand, there is Emile and the war. I am willing to risk my life to put an end to this misery. On the other hand there is my mother, the obligation of maximizing my chances of survival and the promise of a normal, peaceful world.

I will fight. But how? I want to succeed. But how? Wanting something badly enough means getting it. The problem is that I don't know what I want, nor how to go about getting it.

I also answered Elizabeth's letter.

7/6/43

Little Friend,

How are you? Tonight I am all alone. I do not mind. To be by myself for a night or a day and not have to talk to anyone is really what I like best.

I enjoy the leisure to think. My thoughts, however, are not very fruitful and I hurt. I reread your letter dated June 26. So I have to wait a long week before I'll receive your next letter. I would so much like to see you again, even if it were only to argue. I too do not know anyone my own age and am extremely lonely. Every so often, like today, I see Gaby. She comes to town more often now, because she goes to the dentist. From time to time I go to see the mother of Pitt. Don't worry, I am no longer interested in Gert. I don't even want to get even with him. The last year convinced me that small revenges really don't matter. The Germans picked up the family of Roli, his girlfriend, and I feel sorry for her. The H's adopted Roli and treat her as their own child. Recently Roli wrote to forty different concentration camps, trying to locate her parents. If you wish, I'll get you the addresses.

Last week I went to swim at the Saint Sauveur, the first time in a whole year. Many persons would disapprove, because it means taking unnecessary risks. My mother would faint if she knew. I don't think that it was dangerous. I trust my luck and then I believe that my life is not very valuable.

I went to see G, the fat secretary of our school. She is in touch with some of the Jewish students of the lyceé and provides homework. This way they can keep up with their class work. G. is fantastic.

♦

7/7/43

The days drip by as slowly as if they were honey. Today was perfectly awful.

Two months ago I noticed that the workroom above Suzy's
shop was freshly painted. When I visited today, Suzy told me that
Willy decided not to report to the forced-labor camp. I suppose
Willy will stay above her shop. Whatever, Suzy asked me not to
visit anymore and refused to take my letter for Elizabeth. What will
happen to our correspondence? Will I lose her as soon as I found
her again?

Nelly also asked me to come less often. Since Mariette's
arrest, they expect the Germans to come and search their place.

It all makes sense, but . . . I lost the two small havens in my
ocean of loneliness. For once I do not know what to do with
myself. Everything bothers me. I cannot concentrate. I cannot
study. When will all this be over? The last two months were the
worst I can remember, and the end is not in sight.

As recorded, when I delivered the letter to Suzy, she would not take it. I
could not understand why she refused, but in occupied Belgium we all learned
not to question another person's decisions.

8/3/43

I have not written in my diary for an entire month. I even
considered destroying the little notebook. In the end I did not.

Life is intolerably boring. No news about my joining the resistance. Nor are there any other changes except political ones.
Handsome Mussolini said that his health was poor and that he had
to resign.

Mussolini's resignation was only one sign that the tide of the war con-
tinued to shift. By the spring of 1943, the Axis had lost the war in North
Africa, their last troops leaving or surrendeering on May 12. Casualties in
North Africa had been heavy, and we all hoped and expected that Europe
was about to be liberated. Indeed, on July 10, 1943, the Allies landed in
Sicily, and by the end of August the entire island was in their hands.

Sensing defeat, the Italians arrested Mussolini on July 25, 1943, and
initiated peace talks with the Allies. Immediately, Germans troops occupied
the entire Italian peninsula, released Mussolini from his makeshift prison,
and installed him at the head of a puppet government.

◆

At the end of September, I was still at the Vorwindens'. I read, visited friends, and looked for new quarters. To please Tante Bets, I even knitted a sweater from assorted scraps of wool. I still fantasized about Emile, though I sometimes looked at my imaginary love affair with more rational eyes.

9/22/43

My Darling Emile,
Will I ever see you again?
I love you. I love you.
I sometimes think that I dwell on this passion because my life is so empty. Sometimes at night I imagine falling asleep in your arms.
Mon chèri, I know you one whole year already. I wish that I could see you once a month—or even once every two months. If only I could be part of the resistance. Every day, I tell myself that this will come to pass but then nothing happens.
Sometimes I even doubt that I would have the guts to work with you, even if I could.
Bertha told me that Tante Bets slanders me behind my back. The atmosphere here continues to deteriorate. Let me stop writing, otherwise I will again cry my eyes out.

◆

10/2/43

Yesterday Jean and Nelly invited me to celebrate a victory on the Russian Front. Nelly baked a pie. The entire evening was "delicious." I was so happy to be among young people—even though most are ten years older than me.
Emile was at last night's party. I was so shy and tongue-tied that I hardly spoke to him. Gert Ochinsky told me that his parents had been arrested.

In retrospect it is hard to imagine that we were unaware of what was happening to Jews after they were transported "East." Enough people, however, had witnessed the clubs, invectives, and brutality with which the Germans dragged Jews from their homes to realize that capture must be avoided at all costs.

The Jews who were picked up by the Germans were loaded onto trucks and transported to Malines, the Belgian staging camp for deportation. Rumor had it that the fittest "deportees" were separated from the old people, the children, and the sick or disabled. All were then herded aboard freight trains and shipped to the East. As became clear later, using the able-bodied as slave laborers was a minor goal. The major purpose of the mass deportations was the extermination of the Jews. The outside world did not know— or preferred to disbelieve—the facts. Understandably, those of us who were directly concerned could not afford to let our imaginations provide an answer that made sense.

That September the Germans picked up the Belgian Jews who until then had been exempt from deportation. Among these ill-fated were my former neighbors, Miriam and Ala. Miriam, a pretty redhead, was a few years older than I. Like me, she also attended the Lycée de Forest and we sometimes walked home together. She was so polished and proper that I regarded her with admiring awe, never aspiring to be her friend. I did not know her sister, Ala.

When the Germans entered the apartment, they did not arrest the girls' parents, who were Turkish nationals and thus exempt from deportation. The status of the girls, who had been born in Belgium, was unclear. There had been anguished calls to the Turkish consulate, and delays while the pedantic Nazis checked the rules governing this particular case. In the end Miriam and Ala were deported and perished. After the liberation, I gathered my courage and called on their disconsolate, broken parents.

The round-up in Brussels and Antwerp, the last mass arrest of the occupation, netted about fifteen hundred Jews. A handful of Belgian Jews who enjoyed special protection were not arrested. These included "Mon General" Seligman and his cousins, the Van Biemas.

The draft of able-bodied men and selected women—non-Jews—for forced labor in Germany had begun during the fall of 1942. By the summer of 1943, it was in full swing. Many Belgian workers who tried to avoid conscription joined the resistance, hid out in the wooded area of the Ardennes Mountains, escaped continental Europe or lived with friends and relatives. Hundreds of thousands nevertheless ended up in Germany. At the end of the war, a quarter million Belgian slave laborers were working for the Germans.

For young Jews like me, the presence of an ever-increasing pocket of illegals afforded a certain amount of protection. Not only did it overwhelm the German security system, but Jews who were apprehended could pass themselves off as evading Belgian workers and hope to be sent to a labor camp in Germany. This is how Pitt Hirschland survived; the Germans had no idea he was a Jew.

> Today I am blue. I am thinking all the time about Pitt. I turned on the radio, hoping that the music would distract me, but in the middle of the third movement of a Mozart symphony I started to cry. I could not forget anything.
> I am fed up with the war. My favorite phrase is: "It's about time for the war to be over."
> Merde

One of the Vorwindens' neighbors had befriended me. I had told her that I was a distant relative of Tante Bets, but since I had so much trouble finding another shelter, I ended up trusting her and told her the truth. She suggested that I contact one of her friends, a Madame de Groot, who needed help with her three children.

When I reported this new possibility to the Vorwindens, they were so shocked that I had talked to their neighbor that they insisted that I leave after dark that same evening. The last communal dinner in that house was even more chilling than usual.

I packed a few belongings into a small bag—one never traveled with luggage—and went to sleep at my mother's apartment. The next day Madame de Groot interviewed and engaged me as a governess.

Chapter 10

*The Governess of the De Groots** *

Boitsforts, 11/17/43

Mademoiselle Berger, the governess. That's me! Sounds funny. I am taking care of three kids. We'll see how it goes. Life is a bit better, for the time being at least. I enjoy being busy.

My official title at the de Groots' was *governess.* It was better than *maid,* and I felt proud that in spite of my illegal status I had climbed a social ladder of sorts. Actually, soon after I arrived, my new boss fired her maid and I had to do much of the actual housework. The heavy cleaning, however, was done by Marie, a hardworking charwoman.

At the de Groots' I experienced yet another facet of society, totally different from the intellectual left-oriented life at the Wiames' or the secluded, self-centered existence of the Vorwindens. The de Groots were grand, or at least tried to be. They were also disturbed and tense.

A few months earlier, Georges de Groot, the head of household and breadwinner, died after a long and painful struggle with leukemia. Now his family valiantly tried to recover from the emotional roller-coaster accompanying a fatal illness. Madame Ghislaine de Groot, a woman of about forty,

* Not the family's real name.

made a big show of her grief. She wore black, even at home, and billowing widow's weeds whenever she went out.

My charges were Charles, fourteen; Claudette, eight; and Billy, six. All were unusually good-looking. Claudette was dark like her mother, Charles and Billy blond like their father. They were most difficult. Charles, who physically towered over me, refused to listen to his eighteen-year-old governess. He made it clear to his siblings that they need not heed me either.

When his mother went out and I was in charge, Charles delighted in locking me in the cellar or attic. It took all my cunning to foil his plots. Once, when he locked me in a room, I told him through the door that I was happy there since it meant I did not have to work; he, however, was wasting his mother's money. Charles unlocked the door real quick.

My duties included tutoring Charles in German and Flemish, a language in which I had become fluent while at the Vorwindens'. Charles taunted me mercilessly during the tutoring sessions.

Claudette, perhaps as an aftermath of her father's lingering illness, often had nightmares or hallucinations. She screamed—her eyes wide open as if she were awake. Gentle coaxing brought her back to reality. The next day she was sleepy and did even more poorly in school than usual. My helping her with her homework frustrated us both.

Truth, in that house, was a rare commodity. Both Madame and the children were pathological liars. This not only undermined my authority with the children but enraged my Germanic soul. When I reprimanded the children for lying, they said: "Maman lies to you too—you just are too dumb to notice."

Somehow I managed to cope with the children, but not with Ghislaine de Groot. She was unpredictable and constantly blew hot and cold. One day I was her trusted friend, the next I was the worst domestic she had ever had to deal with. She also never paid the miserable allowances she had promised me so that I could pay for my own lunch.

My job involved taking care of the children in the morning: getting them up, feeding them breakfast, and getting them ready for school. The neighbors, who had two children the sames ages as Claudette and Billy, delivered all four youngsters to school. I fetched all four children back after lunch. We took the streetcar. There was no gasoline to operate private cars.

I felt safe shepherding the children around Brussels. It was, however, impossible to distinguish a friendly, joking person from one who might denounce you to the authorities. Once, as I was picking up the four children from school, a man kept staring. I was nervous. In the end he simply said that I must have started having children at a very young age. Another time I forgot the children's lunchbox on the streetcar. I went downtown to the Lost and Found to reclaim it. The clerk in charge examined my papers for a long time. I shook in my boots, but it was a false alarm. The man returned my identity card with a smile, teasingly commenting about having come all the way from Liège to forget my lunch pail on a streetcar in Brussels.

The air war against Germany intensified. All the major cities continued to be bombed regularly. Since Brussels had no heavy industry, it was not an important target, but the hum of airplanes filled the sky at night and then also during the day. The war, and perhaps also the liberation, were coming physically closer.

An occasional stray bomb and the intense activity of the antiaircraft guns added to life's discomfort. One morning Brussels was plastered with a cheerful little rhyme. The following ditty appeared in many parts of town:

The Germans protect us.
The British liberate us.
May God protect us from our liberators,
And liberate us from our protectors.

I remember another happy, war-related event. The Gestapo headquarters in Brussels was housed in a prominent, high-rise sitting at the head of the Avenue Louise. We were all aware of its well-equipped torture chamber, in which the Nazis attempted to extract addresses and other crucial information from their captives. Reports of these interrogations sent chills down the spine of those at risk.

One clear day a single British plane piloted by a Belgian flew so low that it escaped the antiaircraft guns. It located its target on the Avenue Louise, machine-gunned the facade of the Gestapo, and departed before the German planes swung into action. In the week following the attack, thousands of Brussels's citizens filed past the mutilated building, silently expressing their delight at the Germans' discomfiture.

Soon after I arrived at the de Groots', the underground press played a delightful prank on our occupiers. On November 9, 1943, in celebration of the twenty-fifth anniversary of Armistice Day, the Front Indépendent published a newspaper whose format and masthead were an exact replica of *Le Soir,* Brussels's evening paper.

The caper required the cooperation of the Royal Air Force. At the appointed time, Allied planes flew over Brussels, eliciting an air alert that delayed delivery of the regular edition of *Le Soir.* During that time cyclists of the resistance delivered the "fake *Soir*" to newsstands throughout the city. People who picked up the paper on their way home from work were astounded to read that the Germans admitted to having lost the war, that the bread rations were increased, and that Germany was reeling from the air war.

The fake *Soir* immediately became a collector's item, copies selling for as much as one thousand francs, swelling the needy coffers of the underground. In spite of ever-increasing hardships, the mood in Brussels was up.

As 1943 turned into 1944, I spent one more New Year's Eve at the Salomons, unhappily feeling that my life was slipping by. Would I turn into an old maid before I ever had a chance to go out with boys?

January 1944
The first month of a new year, what will it bring? I can't stand
to live with people who supposedly are my friends, but are not.
I hate people mixing into everybody else's business. It is easier
to besmirch than to admire or simply to take care of one's own
affairs.

While the de Groot children were in school, my time was my own. I still hoped to fill it with useful work for the resistance. In the meantime I amused myself as best I could. As always, reading was my favorite escape.

January, 1944
This noon, before picking the kids up from school, I visited a
bookstore. I would readily give a year of my life if I could buy all
the books I want to own.
I managed to subscribe to a lending library and now can
borrow books. I read several awful ones, including one by

Casanova. To cheer myself up I borrowed "Les Thibaults." I still love it and am discovering new depths. [This ten volume epic recounts the life of two brothers, Antoine and Jacques Thibault, before, during, and after World War I.]

My chief interest at the de Groots' was my continued first-hand investigation of the social strata. Madame de Groot did not rate very high.

Madame de Groot has serious troubles—at least she thinks that her problems are serious. Apparently somebody is gossiping behind her back, implying that she was unfaithful to her dear, departed husband.

She keeps telling me about it. The story is already coming out of my ears! People often confide in me. I don't like it at all.

I would so much like to act—to use my strength—do something—spend myself. I have no outlet.

The plight of the cleaning woman was closer to my heart. Marie, a devout Catholic, felt that heaven would repay her for her earthly woes: the whims of the rich, an alcoholic husband, a clutch of ungrateful brats. Listening to her stories convinced me that the existing social order needed revision.

Marie, the cleaning woman of the de Groots, also tells me of her misfortunes. Today she complained about the unfairness of her employers.

"They waste millions, and never work. I work all the time, and never have a penny.

"Take my Mademoiselle Eveline, for example.

"In the morning she gets up at 10 or 10:30. Then she distributes soup to the poor, then she lunches. Then off to the movies or the theater. Then it is tea and pastries which tide her over to dinner. A nice life, would you not say?" Yet, according to Marie, Mademoiselle Eveline is not even happy.

I wonder whether "happy people" and "happiness" exist? The rich are afraid to lose their money; the poor work like dogs to make ends meet.

◆

One can divide people into those who have a heart and those who have money. If given a choice, I would pick a heart.

Just look at the difference between Delphine Bellins, the simple ex-nun who sheltered my mother, and my Ghislaine! After living with that bitch for three months, I still feel completely ill at ease in her house.

If I could only be a member of the resistance and work with Emile . . .

If only I had a lover.

If only my days were filled with activity.

If only . . .

The importance the de Groots attached to outward appearances disturbed me greatly. To them it was of the utmost importance who invited whom with whom, when, and where.

And so Madame de Groot gave a dinner party. She confided that some people criticized her for entertaining so soon after her husband's death. She felt the dinner was simply a thank-you for the support her friends had given her during Georges's long illness.

The party was most elegant. Ghislaine hired a cook and two waiters. During the day, provisions arrived and the guests sent beautiful and elaborate flower arrangements delivered by Brussels' leading florists. The table gleamed with crystal and silver. In the evening, before dinner, I dressed Claudette and Billy in their Sunday best. They went downstairs, curtsied or bowed, then I put them to bed and retired to my little room on the top floor of the house, envying the dinner guests' laughter and the fine food.

The next morning I got some of the leftovers. Then Ghislaine and her mother took all the flowers to Georges's grave to "thank him for the fabulous wines from the cellar he so lovingly assembled." To me the whole affair smacked of a cheap novel.

When I first went to see Madame de Groot, I told her that I was from Liège—as my false papers indicated— and that I was avoiding conscription by the Germans. It did not take her very long to discover that I was escaping more than forced labor. Once she figured out that I was Jewish, she had

mixed feelings about my presence in her house. Since I worked hard and did
my job well, I did not comprehend her changed attitude and was mystified
by her increasing abuse.

2/4/44

Gee-whiz! Last night Madame de Groot told me:
"I prefer that you do not talk to me.
"I simply keep you out of the goodness of my heart.
"I feed you without stamps [not true]—you don't do a stitch of
work all day long.
"I could manage better with a governess who would be here
only from four o'clock in the afternoon to seven in the evening.
"Jews are all the same . . . it does not pay to be nice to them."
She had never mentioned me being Jewish before, and I did
not tell her. What shall I do now?

♦

2/5/44

A good book is a real comfort when life is hard and sad. I
discovered Zola and devour his novels.

I still had not forgotten Emile:

2/17/44

Emile, my little boy,
Since I am here at the de Groots', I love you even more than
before. I have never met anyone as rich, as nasty, and as stupid
as the de Groots. Is there really no way in which I could help win
this war?
Today Madame G made another scene and fired me. Merde.
Only the little girl, Claudette, is sad about my leaving. She told
me that her mother is mean. It made me feel good.
Life here will be hell until I depart. I wish that I could leave
tomorrow. What a luxury to always say what one thinks. To do that,
I guess one must be very rich or very independent. Certainly one
cannot be Jewish and hide from the Germans.
Down with compromise. Down, down!

When I leave here I'll tell G that she will have to look far and wide before finding anyone else like me.

Shit!

♦

2/18/44

Well, I thought a lot about the situation here and believe that I finally figured it out. About three weeks ago Madame G talked about me to one of her friends. That person might have pointed out that sheltering Jews is a criminal offense that might land her in jail.

Since then she looked for a pretext to give me the sack. In a way, she is scared to keep me and afraid to fire me. Knowing her, she does not even want to admit her fear to herself.

This morning after breakfast G apologized, and told me to pay no attention to what she said yesterday. She blamed her nerves and her hairdresser who kept her for hours. During the rest of the day she was particularly pleasant.

In spite of Madame de Groot's more positive attitude, I decided to look for another hiding place. I returned to the employment agency and they sent me on interviews. I also alerted my friends.

2/24/44

I phoned Nelly and she implied that she might have found a new place for me. Hurrah! I became hopeful and excited.

Emile, today is the twenty-sixth anniversary of the founding of the Red Army.

♦

2/25/44

I am still rereading "Les Thibaults." I suppose that most young adults are ashamed of their feelings. The letters that Antoine and Jacques Thibault exchanged are not all that different from my own scribblings.

Only, I must deal with all this shit by myself. I am very tired. I am relieved each evening when the day is over. I am also terribly scared.

◆

2/27/44

Another Sunday! I have been here for four months! G makes my life miserable. Even with the children, she provides no support and undermines my authority. She criticizes me in front of Claudette, Billy, and Charles, and I have trouble making them do their chores.

Part of the trouble is that we have different ideas about what is important. The old goat does not care whether her children lie or not. She cares only about appearances.

Without outside interference I manage. Today I took care of my two little ones and the two brats from next door. Everybody had a good time.

I wish that I could talk my problems over with Elizabeth. Life is so complicated and I am unable to sort it out all by myself.

◆

2/28/44

Bless Nelly. I visited her today and we talked. What I said might not have made much sense. I do not yet dare talk to Nelly as if she were my friend. Perhaps I will be able to someday.

Nelly was especially kind tonight. I made a mess of the potatoes for the soup, and she simply laughed. If the Wiames only knew how important they are to me.

◆

2/29/44

Today I did something real stupid. I locked Charles's study with a key and forgot to open it when I left. I was not home when Charles came back, and he could not enter his room. Madame G was beside herself with rage.

"I really think that I—" she said, then she stopped. I am sorry that I did not finish the sentence for her. I suppose she wanted to say ". . . will give you notice." Next time I hope to be quicker on my feet. If only I could find another job, one that would leave me some free time to work for the resistance.

Because I could not leave before I actually found another shelter I poured my anger out in my diary:

◆

2/29/44

Madame Ghislaine:

I am leaving. Yes, I am leaving. I hope that you are surprised. You believed that I would take everything. Well, you were wrong.

I am going because I am not a dog and do not wish to be treated like one. I am not quitting because I have to work too hard. You could have given me twice as much work, and I would have stayed. I am leaving because you are nasty, petty, demanding, and self-indulgent. You think that one can buy everything. Well, my pet, things of real value cannot be bought.

You do not have a single real friend. You pay your friends, and they pay you back. A smile, buys a smile; a dinner invitation buys a dinner invitation; flowers buy flowers.

If you were to lose your money, you would be all alone. You are unhappy now and never were happy. You were never young, and keep your children from being young, carefree, and relaxed. Instead of giving them love, you stifle them with toys and other material possessions. You are a fool, and deep down you must know it. You have no backbone. You waver and hesitate and want people to believe that you are firm and powerful. You are selfish, but want others to think that you are generous.

◆

3/1/44

Wow, how mad I was when I wrote last! I thought it was at least original, but today I read something like it in Bernard Shaw.

◆

3/4/44

When I came home last night a drunk boarded my streetcar. He looked around and sat next to me. I am terrified of drunks, even though this guy was rather likable and good-looking. He said that he loved me and that I was beautiful. This was a new experience. How I wish that he had been sober.

Then the guy started to insult the Germans. My panic increased. What if there was a pro-Nazi aboard who wished to make trouble?

Finally I got up and changed seats. The drunk became even more indignant, telling me that I would have flirted with him had he been a German soldier.

If he only knew! I wonder whether I liked him because he flattered me or because he had the nerve to state his political views out loud? Once in my life I too would like to be slightly drunk.

◆

I went to an interview about a job in Droogenbosch. There are five children and the woman is pregnant. I would like the job, but would be too busy to work for the resistance.

My mom wanted to come visit here today. But there was an air-raid alert and she had to cancel.

Ghislaine got more friendly.

◆

3/5/44

2 P.M.: I told Madame de Groot that I was leaving. Now that's done with.

Evening: All strong emotions, even when painful or scary, are precious. If only I had succeeded to work for the resistance when I first came here! By now I would have spent four months doing that.

I had a long talk with Ghislaine this afternoon. I had been correct in my assessment of the situation. When I told her that I planned to leave, she suddenly became much more pleasant. For some reason she felt that she could not ask me to leave. Perhaps indeed she feared that there might be reprisals later on. So she made my life miserable and I had no choice but to quit. Whatever, G continues to fabricate stories about me which are duly reported by the children or the cleaning woman. The latest tales are that I rummage through her packages and blow my nose into her handkerchiefs!

◆

3/9/44

Uncertainty, rage, and yet somehow I feel calm. I don't seem to care anymore. I must be getting used to living with fear. Until the end of the month I have a roof, and then we'll see. I wonder about Emile. I called Nelly, but there was no news. How I wish things would turn out well once in a while.

◆

3/10/44

Another day gone by. I hurt. When I feel like this the smallest, most unimportant incident makes me burst into tears.

The Wiames think it might be safe for me to come back. Funny, now I am not sure that I want to return there. I really don't know why. I love all of them. They are the most admirable people I know. So why don't I want to go?

At night I am so tired that I am afraid I'll fall asleep standing up. Tonight fortunately, I do not have to wash myself. Since there is no one to care for me I give myself a little pep talk:

"Come on, little one, get going; soon you will be in bed."

Washing oneself in war-deprived Belgium was most unpleasant. The bathroom was ice cold, and there was no hot water. There also was no soap. Other everyday necessities were nonexistent as well. Shoes had wooden soles, and I badly needed a new winter coat. Fabric was available on the black market. Madame de Groot's black garments were certainly new and elegant.

3/14/44

The news from the front are vague and odd. The Germans talk of an "elastic front, a swiveling offensive, sealing off enemy break-throughs, disengagement maneuvers, and defensive victories . . ." To me it sounds good.

The war indeed was progressing well. In January 1944 the Russians broke the Leningrad blockade. By March they were on the offensive in the Ukraine and started to reconquer the Crimea.

My mother had located another illegal apartment. The indefatigable Mr. Salomon had approached Madame Lebacqz, the widow of yet another of his former clients.

After her husband died, Madame Lebacqz and her scientist son continued to live in the elegant one-family house. When the son married an American woman, Mrs. Lebacqz lodged the young couple in a small apartment on the third floor of her house. Then the son and his wife left for California. His mother and her dog, Toto, remained alone in the big house in Brussels.

When Mr. Salomon asked her whether she would rent the now-empty apartment to my mother, she agreed even though her immediate neighbors included some Gestapo officers. In spite of her innate reserve, Madame Lebacqz and my mother became friends. Eventually Gaby and I would develop a special bond with the elderly lady whose grace and dignity were at variance with the incomprehensible, berserk world in which we all lived.

My mother's apartment was cozy and nicely furnished. It fronted on a small lake. When bored we watched the ducks. I loved visiting, especially since I was so unhappy living at the de Groots'. I wish that I could stay home, but for the time being it was safer for me to return to my hateful job.

3/16/44

Indecision, rage. Emile!

Last night I dreamt of him. What I remember best is his eyes. They are lively, cold, and mocking. Their effect on me is quite unpredictable. They chill me to the bone or rekindle my strength and courage. When he is around, my brain seems to work a bit faster. When I see him I can even be witty.

Still, this make-believe affair with Emile is quite ludicrous. Should I abandon it?

◆

Today I won a fight with Charles. A stray cat entered the kitchen and devoured the leftover roast beef. Charles said that the cat got in through the bathroom window that I had left open! I proved that the cat entered by the kitchen window and that it thus could not be my fault. I briefly considered making a fuss about being wrongly accused again, but what is the use. It would only backfire.

◆

Yesterday I visited Jacqueline Corvillain, [René] Fuss's sister. She is a bit older than me and was my chieftaine [leader] at the Girl Scouts. Now she is married and already has a baby! Jacqueline has a friend who needs a "chambermaid." I'll go for an interview tomorrow.

◆

I am such a fool. Since more than a year I badly want to get more friendly with Suzy Anciaux, a friend of Jean and Nelly. Suzy is Jewish. She and Gert Ochinsky want to get married but can't because Suzy cannot divorce her non-Jewish husband. Well, yesterday I saw Suzy on the streetcar and was too shy to say hello.

♦

3/17/44

Yesterday I went to talk to Jacqueline's friend. The woman seems nice enough, but I would hate to be a real chambermaid. Will I take the job if she offers it to me? Probably not. It would mean abandoning my dream of working for the resistance; forgetting Emile completely, and giving up being "Mademoiselle Berger, the governess." It would mean waiting at the table and being obsequious.

Perhaps it would do me good; perhaps it would teach me to be a "good" revolutionary.

It all made me cry.

♦

3/18/44

The soap one gets with food stamps is almost pure mud. When used, it leaves a brown stain on the clothes and hands. Since its main ingredient is clay, the manufacturer confidently states that he will be able to supply the country with this soap until doomsday.

♦

3/21/44

I visited Nelly who now lives with her mother in the ancestral home in which she and Emile grew up. The house felt very peaceful. I wish that I could stay there, in a little corner, until the war is over.

During my visit Nelly phoned some friends and in "double-talk" asked whether they could use me. I gather that she gave me a fairly good recommendation.

Nelly's friendliness cheered me up. Even Mrs. Altorfer was nice. They cannot possibly know how important this is for me right now. I could never get by without their support.

Perhaps every adolescent worships somebody or something. I have an overabundance of passion and no outlet. I need to love, to give of myself, but how?

I lost my self-confidence, my peace of mind, my faith. I even doubt that we will win this war. I no longer can look people straight in the eye. When will this nightmare end?

The Russians are six hundred miles from Berlin. If they advance six miles each day they will reach Berlin in one hundred days. Hurrah, hurrah. Emile, I love you with all my heart and soul. Each day I love you a bit more. Why are you married? Why are you so old? I am afraid. I hope that nothing will happen to you.

Enough scribbling for tonight. I must clean my shoes; after that, I'll read Bernard Shaw.

◆

3/22/44

Boy, Ghislaine is really mean—she is an idiot. I think that she is jealous of the way I handle the kids.

Tonight she would not even loan me the newspaper, even though she was expecting company for bridge and had no time to read it.

Ghislaine told me to help Charles with his German homework. He won't listen to me, claiming that I don't know any German!

I wish that I was strong enough not to care about people like the de Groots and their petty stuff.

I am here only for another ten days. I have not yet found another hiding place. It turns out that I cannot return to the Wiames' after all. I'll find something at the last minute.

◆

3/23/44

To be alone.

Emile.

To love, and not hate, and never grow old.

Today I waited for the streetcar stop in front of the university. I tried to imagine what you were like when you were a student.

Will I even go back to school?

When I lived in Auderghem with the Wiames and the Vorwindens, I often took a streetcar that ambled to town along the Avenue de Tervuren. There I had always admired a low-slung modern house, set back in a magnificent garden. When it turned out to be the house the employment agency sent me to, my expectations were high.

Madame Jacqueline Grosfils needed a governess for her three older children—Jean-Pierre, age seven; Monique, age six; and Claudine, age five. She also wanted some help with six-month-old Martine, for whom she cared mostly herself.

In view of my bad experience at the de Groots, I told Madame Grosfils that I was Jewish, had decent false papers, would provide my own food stamps, and was willing to work for free.

Though Madame Grosfils liked me, she said that she had to check with her husband. I received a positive answer the next day. I was to start work on April 1, April Fools' Day.

3/27/44

I am cross today. I leave here Friday night. Monday morning I start working for a Madame Jean Grosfils. I had hoped to have a little vacation and spend some time at home.

I guess one is never satisfied. First I was worried not finding a roof. Now I mind having found one too quickly. Ghislaine de Groot is an old goat. She says she found a new governess. I wonder how long she will stay?

♦

3/28/44

I am sad, disgusted, and distraught.

♦

3/31/44

GOOD-BYE, GHISLAINE.

Chapter 11

Dawn

To my utter delight, my new job started with a two-week sojourn in Baisey, a small village not too far from Brussels, where the Grosfils family owned a working farm. My new employers traveled by car, but I was told to take the train. The ride was an adventure.

April 1944

When I arrived at the station, the train was so full that I boarded the freight car. The train stayed in the station forever. Finally the train left, but almost immediately the air-raid sirens started to blare. The train stopped and we all got off. After the all clear, I climbed back onto my freight car and we were on our way. Five minutes later there was another alert. It took hours to cover a distance of about twenty-five miles. The ride, at least, was free. The conductor never managed to collect the fare.

The train ride was an example of the increasing disarray of everyday life. The constant air alerts frayed nerves, and we all expected the Allies to liberate us, but our wait seemed futile.

♦

I had not left Brussels for two years and had forgotten that country roads, wheat fields, meadows studded with spring flowers, haylofts, and barns full of mooing cows even existed. My enthusiasm for the farm was contagious, and I made friends with my new little charges. We spent the days exploring the farm. We saw how churning turned milk into mouth-watering yellow butter, and how the eggs were candled, the cows milked, and the horses harnessed to wagons. We played hopscotch, blind man's bluff, hide-and-seek, and other games. We took crayons outdoors, drew pictures, and read picture books. My spirits were up.

In the evening after I tucked the children into bed, I roamed the country roads on a borrowed bicycle, filling my lungs with fresh air. Had peace returned?

One of the local attractions was an American aircraft that had force-landed in an isolated field near Baisey. Everyone went to see this tangible sign of Allied strength and approaching salvation. One evening I too bicycled over to inspect the aircraft. I saw the silvery plane, with its thirty-five-meter wingspan from afar.

When I got closer I realized the folly of my errand. Two German soldiers guarded the plane. Their smirks and inviting faces left little doubt of their interest in the buxom, redheaded visitor.

One of the soldiers took me into the cockpit and cabin. The panel was completely stripped of its instruments by the German intelligence service, which delighted in this unexpected catch. I breathed a sigh of relief when my summary inspection was over and I reemerged from the bowel of the plane unscathed. My guide then took me to see the mascot, a curvaceous nude pin-up girl, painted on the fuselage. "Let's do like her," he suggested. "Nein," I said in German disguised with a heavy French accent, "my mother is waiting." The soldier did not insist. I grabbed my bike and pedalled off. I was proud to have seen the plane, but once more remorseful of having taken unnecessary risks. I'll be more careful next time," I swore to myself.

I had won the confidence of Madame Grosfils and formed strong bonds with the children by the time we all returned to Brussels. I quickly settled into the complex Grosfils household. I shared a room with Claudine, and that interfered with my reading of the many interesting books I found at the Grosfils'.

I met my new boss, Monsieur Grosfils, who had not shared our vacation. He was a slight, energetic man. Like my father, his short stature bothered him and to compensate he carried himself very erect. Like Emile, he had entered the family business, in this case a large brewery; also like my love, he considered this somewhat of a burden. After the war he hoped to start publishing a liberal Catholic newspaper. Monsieur Grosfils had visited America and loved New York.

Madame Grosfils's father had founded one of the early rayon mills in Belgium. He was proud of having done his share in decreasing the cost of the silklike fabric so the poorer people could afford to buy quality clothes at reasonable prices.

I was happier at the Grosfils' than I had been since I left the Wiames'. Nevertheless, my very well-defined position in that household bothered me. Madame Grosfils asked me to wear a coif and a white uniform so I would look the part of the proper, high-class governess. I rebelled at the headdress, claiming that it kept sliding off my voluminous hair.

The children were my pass to social acceptability. When they were around, I ate with the family and used the front gate. When alone, I had to use the servants' entrance. When there was company, I delivered the spruced-up children to the living room and picked them up some ten minutes later.

My social position was thus halfway between that of an equal and a domestic. This made my life difficult with the other employees. I did not mind the distance between me and Jeanne, the cook, an old shrew whom I avoided as much as possible. She delighted in telling me dirty stories that clearly shocked and embarrassed me. When she could she pinched my breasts or my behind. But I really liked Gina. We hid our friendship from Madame Grosfils, who disapproved of her governess hobnobbing with her chambermaid.

Gina, a true redhead, was most attractive. She had grown up in a small Belgian mining town. Now, at twenty-five, she desperately wanted to settle down and have a family of her own. On her day off she frequented various dance halls; she met men who promised marriage, but really only wanted to bed her down. "Experienced" me advised her on her prospects and suggested appropriate courses of action. The countless women's magazines read at the Vorwindens now paid off.

For Gina I fabricated all kinds of lies to explain my presence at the Grosfils. She wanted to know why I did not look for a man. Why did I run back to my mama on my day off instead of going dancing with her?

♦

The elegant Grosfils home was built on a corner lot. A large garden shielded the front of the house, but the service wing fronted directly onto a side street. Most mornings I watched a platoon of twenty German soldiers, dressed in ordinary loden-green uniforms, march down this street. They sang about birds, flowers, sweethearts, fidelity, love, and loss. How could they reconcile the savagery of their war with their German romanticism and sentimentality? How could they be so content? I recognized many of the songs. My grandfather had liked to sing the one about two comrades who had fought together in World War I. I had always loved the one about the lonely rose blooming on the heath. In spite of my hatred and fear, my heart responded to the melodies and the sweet words resonated in my memory.

In May 1944 the Allies repeatedly bombed Brussels, the attacks centering on the enormous freight yard and locomotive repair shop. Eventually, the planes leveled the yard, the shop, and a good number of locomotives and freight and passenger cars. Hundreds of civilians were killed, wounded, or rendered homeless. Smoke from the burning houses darkened the sky. The authorities thought it prudent to close the school. Madame Grosfils and I started to teach the children at home, and I was in my glory.

My mother felt that since nobody went to school, it would be safe for her fourteen-year-old school-age daughter to live with her. So my sister bid her hosts farewell and returned to Brussels. On my day off, I now visited with my mother and Gaby.

At the Grosfils', it took the strength of four adults—Madame, Jeanne, Gina, and myself—to run a household with four small children. I enjoyed making myself indispensable and assumed jobs that strictly speaking did not fall into the province of a governess. One of these was making bread.

The commercially available bread, baked from flour mixed with all kinds of junk, was practically inedible. Even when fresh it had an obnoxious, foul smell. Once a week I stood in line at the bakery and exchanged our bread stamps for flour. Back home I sifted it several times to separate out the bran and other fillers. Then Jeanne added some black-market flour and yeast, kneaded the dough, and let the bread rise twice in fourteen separate pans—two for each day of the week. I cycled the leavened loaves, carefully shielded by towels to prevent them from catching cold, to the bakery for baking. It took three separate trips to deliver the unbaked loaves. Several hours later my trusty bicycle and I fetched the bread home.

Most evenings Monsieur Grosfils invited me into the living room to listen to *Radio Londres*. The broadcast concluded with a long string of coded messages such as: *Six friends will come tonight, the cat is chasing its tail,* and *tell your mother to hang up the wash.* Some of these messages were obviously for the resistance fighters hidden throughout Western Europe. Others were meaningless, designed to keep the Germans in a constant state of alert and confusion.

By the spring of 1944, even the local newspapers felt that the Allied invasion of France was imminent. The Germans prepared for the event by fortifying their "invulnerable Atlantic Wall" along the coasts of Holland, Belgium, and France. The dunes and beaches were riddled with bunkers, pillboxes, tank traps, and barbed wire. Mines studded the underwater approaches and the shore.

Fortunately, the Allies managed to keep the date of the actual invasion a secret. They also deceived the Germans as to the site of the landing. Therefore, on June 6, 1944, D-Day, the Allies initially met only a fraction of the sixty divisions with which the Germans planned to "throw the attackers back into to ocean."

News of the landing spread across Belgium instantly. People abandoned all sense of caution and gathered around open windows where someone was listening to the BBC: "They've come, at last; by boat. They've released thousands of parachutes." Eventually, General Dwight Eisenhower, the commander of the expedition, addressed continental Europe; Belgium's prime-minister-in-exile cautioned his compatriots to be calm.

That evening the official press reported that the Allies disembarked in Normandy. *Le Soir* stressed the heavy losses suffered by the "enemy" and "reassured" us that the British and Americans were considering abandoning their foothold.

Later we learned that during the carefully planned "Operation Overlord," British troops landed in Normandy between Arromanches-les-Bains and Cabourg, on beaches dubbed Gold, Juno, and Sword. Using their traditional determination, the British were to hold these beachheads at all costs.

The Americans, with talent for mobile warfare, landed a little farther West, near Sainte-Mère-Église. From these sites, designated Utah Beach and Omaha Beach, they dashed inland as far and as fast as they could. Losses, especially of American troops, were extremely heavy, but the success of Overlord surpassed all expectations. By nightfall 145,000 soldiers were ashore.

Six days later, on the twelfth, 326,547 soldiers, 54,196 vehicles, and 104,428 tons of equipment were ashore.

An air of joyous expectation pervaded Brussels as we greeted the news of the Allied advances. It was almost as if we could hear the noise of the still-distant battle. The agony, however, was far from over. Actually, for those living underground, the events in Belgium took an unexpected turn for the worse. General Alexander von Falkenhausen, the comparatively benign commander of northern France and Belgium, was arrested in June 1944 for being too lenient and sent to Dachau. The administration in Brussels was now headed by the ex-mayor of Cologne, an especially devoted Nazi, assisted by a vulture of a police chief.

On June 8, two days after D-Day, King Leopold III and his immediate family were transferred from their castle in Brussels to Germany. Since the king's behavior was questioned by many patriots, there was talk that he was afraid of the reaction of his subjects once they were liberated. The official story was that "the Germans evacuated the king because they could no longer guarantee his safety." After the war the country was so divided about the ambiguous role Leopold had played during the war that after years of controversy he abdicated in favor of his son Baudouin.

Given the extreme labor shortage, the Germans redoubled their efforts of rounding up those who dodged their forced-labor drafts. German patrol cars circulated through town, checking the identity papers of all likely candidates. Few of these, however, were in plain view. They stayed home or hid out in the countryside, especially in the Ardennes Mountains.

The Germans redoubled their efforts against the resistance. Sabotage increased, as did summary execution of hostages and other prisoners.

Brussels was nevertheless permeated with an air of happy expectation. By late June, after months of bombing and constant alerts, the antiaircraft guns were silent. Hundreds of low-flying Allied bombers filled the sky but passed unmolested. Spring had finally arrived. The sun was shining as it had four years earlier when all this madness began. Cautiously, everyone ventured outside, strolling along the wide chestnut tree-lined avenues and in Brussels's many parks.

♦

7/1/44

Public transportation in Brussels is in total disarray. On Sundays the streetcars do not run at all. For three weeks we had no telephone because the Germans feared another landing by the Allies. Now the telephone service is restored. The Germans need manpower desperately and are pissed off. They arrest lots of young men and young girls on the streets.

My little charges are very sweet. They adore me and I love them back. I hardly see anybody else. I enjoy being busy and hope that school will stay closed. I would miss the children during the day.

♦

7/3/44

I am more cheerful, less discouraged, and I know why. I finally got my period. [I had not menstruated for nine months, probably because I was malnourished.] I also was hurt when Jacqueline Grosfils sent me upstairs when her parents came to visit. I cried. Gina, the chambermaid, came up and consoled me.

I heroically resolved not to lick other people's plates anymore. I wonder how long I will be able to keep that promise? Perhaps forever.

Tomorrow I have my day off and will go home. I hope that Mom won't harp about the arrests the Germans make in the streets and other true and false rumors.

♦

At dinner the other night, Monsieur Grosfils commented on the fact that black soldiers are sent to Europe to kill whites. This prompted seven-year-old Jean-Pierre to expound on his view of the world:

"Africa is a good country. They have plenty of food, and sleep a lot. France is a big country, with no food, no sleep and lots of boum-boum.

"The Allies don't like to come here to Belgium, because at home they have no war. We don't care, we are used to the boum-boums."

Emile was still in my thoughts:

♦

7/7/44

Good evening, my love. I feel lousy. I regret more and more that I did not try harder to work for the resistance. I visited the parents of Jean Wiame. They are simple blue-collar workers who say what they think and are honest. I can't stand all the hypocrites I live with. I want to love and be loved.

♦

7/9/44

Today I thought that the Germans arrested my Mom and Gaby. I called Madame Lebacqz and she said they were gone. I ran everywhere to locate them: the Salomons, Corvillain, the Hirschlands. I wondered what I could do. I imagined them being in the cellar of the Gestapo, on Avenue Louise, and tried to remember what Dr. Hertz had said about getting them out of there. I thought about taking a leave from my job here. To do what? I now wonder. The unknown is terribly hard to bear.

Dr. Hertz, our doctor, continued to see his patients, many of whom now were illegal. Whenever we had a medical problem, my mother and I consulted him in his home-office, still protected by the official seal of the Italian embassy. We also continued to see our dentist, who even made orthodontic braces for my sister.

Dr. Hertz was a sly old bird. He had befriended the Gestapo by exchanging postage stamps with one official and playing cards with another. He used these connections, when necessary, to have some of his friends and patients released from their temporary quarters in the basement of the Gestapo on Avenue Louise. He had told my mother to contact him immediately should the need arise. Once a prisoner was transferred elsewhere, Hertz's connections were powerless.

That morning in my panic, I tried calling Dr. Hertz. Fortunately, the phone did not work:

7/9/44

The whole thing turned out to be a misunderstanding. Mom and Gaby simply went for a long walk in the country.

♦

7/20/44

Today some German generals tried to assassinate Hitler. The coup failed. The bastard is lucky!

News from the front could not be better. The Russians are ten kilometers from the border of East Prussia. They launched an offensive near Lvov. There is a new offensive in Normandy. The Allies march up the Italian peninsula. Ancona and Livorno fell.

Life here is the same. I am reading André Malraux's *Man's Hope,* his book about the Spanish Civil War. My little charges are very charming. They went back to school and I have more free time. The three older ones listen to me, and I manage better with Claudine. Yesterday I dropped the baby!

Jacqueline Grosfils is in a very bad mood these days! I wish they would all leave me be.

I phoned Madame Nelly. She was supportive, as always. For the first time I sensed that she was eager that I come to visit.

Next Saturday the Grosfils are giving a big dinner to celebrate July 21, the Belgian Independence Day, the victories in Normandy, and the crossing of the German border by Russian troops.

Jacqueline asked whether I could sleep somewhere else that night.

I decided that if I ever have a son, I'll call him Emile.

◆

7/23/44

The big dinner here with a lot of tra la la was yesterday. There were sixteen guests. Because of the curfew everybody slept over at the Grosfils' house. Juliette, the cook of Madame Grosfils's mother, was in charge of the kitchen; Jeanne was furious.

I had done a lot of shopping for the party. I bought wild strawberries at Bernard, Brussels's fanciest caterer. That store has everything from soup to nuts: caviar, sausages, fruit. To think that the war has been going on for five years! All one needs is pots of money. In this case the guests split the cost of the groceries.

I went to fetch a kettle big enough to cook French fries for twenty from Jacqueline's brother, Andrew F. With his blond curly hair, blue eyes, and dark skin, he is the most handsome guy I ever met. I suppose he is what one describes as being "macho."

Jeanne and Gina were very upset that I had been asked to leave after I put the kids to bed and before the dinner was served. So Jeanne sneaked me some French fries and other treats. When I came back early the next morning to take charge of the kids, she welcomed me with some wine and scraps of dessert. Actually, I had welcomed my unexpected free night. The joyous noise of the party would have made me feel like a third-rate Cinderella.

7/28/44

Despair, courage, but life rolls on. I have many real dreams, not only daydreams. One day, I hope to accomplish something. I would hate to spend my life vegetating. The more I know, the more lost and confused I feel. There is good and bad everywhere.

Time rushes by and memories fade quickly. The de Groot children, Claudette and Billy, already vanished from my mind.

♦

8/6/44

Life is dull, nothing happens. I have no pep and feel tired. I fought with Gina. Yesterday I visited Marie, the cleaning woman of the de Groots. I volunteered to mend her family's socks and took an enormous bunch with me. Why on earth did I do that? Now I am sorry I did.

The bicycle with which I rendered the Grosfils family so many important services also became my temporary passport to freedom. I had received my first bicycle when I was ten. I used it to escape from the grayness of everyday life. I daydreamed as I rode through the woods near my old house in Hanover or, later, in Brussels's Forêt de Soignes. A bicycle was a convenient mode of transportation, and I grievously missed mine after I had gone underground.

Now that I again had a bicycle, I often took it out when my time was my own. I usually went for a spin, across the street from the Grosfils' in the Parc de Woluwé, the very same park that had also abutted the Vorwindens' house.

One evening that summer, I came across a group of fifteen adults and children playing volleyball. I got off my bike, watching hungrily as the ball flew back and forth across the net. I felt like Alice in Wonderland coming across the queen's croquet game.

"You want to play?" one of the adults asked me. He used the familiar French form of address and was the obvious leader of the little group.

"Yes," I answered without hesitation. "What's your name," the man asked.

"Suzanne," I said. That was about the extent of our conversation. Nobody ever asked me for my last name, where I lived, or what I was doing. I never learned who the players were. This was wartime etiquette. I returned the following week, same time, same place. My magic game was there, and I joined one of the teams. I happily ran around for an hour, hitting the ball as best I could. The game became the highlight of my week; it was the promise of a return to a more normal existence.

Chapter 12

Of Heaven and Hell

As the end of the war approached, the Nazis and collaborators became more ferocious. Suzy Tamineau's fiance, Willy, was arrested for evading labor conscription. In mid-August Nelly told me that Emile too had disappeared. Though my passion for him had abated, the news of his arrest threw me into deep despair and rekindled my infatuation. I also knew how terrible the loss was for Nelly, Mrs. Altorfer, and Mariette and Annie.

8/17/44

My Poor Chèri,

I cannot fathom it! My senses are completely dulled. You are the one I loved most among those this war is destroying. Yet, when Nelly told me that you had "vanished," I was less shocked then when I learned about Mariette and Pitt. I probably cannot yet cope with the pain and am displacing it.

Perhaps the report is false. No, I engage in wishful thinking. My antenna is quite acurate. Poor Nelly. Your poor mother, and your poor little Annie.

We must work hard to replace all of you.

◆

I am frightened, but the more afraid I am the more indifferent and detached I feel.

Emile, I made a vow, and not for the first time. Remember when you and Jean taunted me because I am such a mess-pot? Since then I always clean up my room. I'll try to continue. I'll always be neat for you.

I hope that you won't be tortured. I am terrified for you!

Good night, mon cheri. Sleep well, and sometimes think of me.

◆

The Americans now advance rapidly from Normandy toward Brittany, Rennes, Nantes, Chartres, Orléans, and, best of all, Paris. Allegedly one can hear cannon fire in Paris. There was a second Allied landing in southern France, between Cannes and Toulon.

In the East the rapid progress of the Red Army came to a halt. Finally, however, the Russians liberated Warsaw. On the 17th of August the Russians penetrated heavily defended eastern Prussia. The Vaterland defended its soil vigorously.

◆

The Nazis arrest and execute all the German generals who partook in the coup against Hitler. Those executed include the nephew of General von Falkenhausen, who governed us during the past four years and to whom we owe a relatively mild persecution.

Hitler delighted in hanging von Falkenhausen and the other conspirators "naked, like cattle." So many generals have been executed that one jokes that the Nazis run advertisements for new ones.

◆

8/22/44

Today I seem to have gone off my rocker. Last night I slept very little, and then I thought about Emile, and I was hungry.

The evening before, I had to babysit and could not go play volleyball which had become my only social outlet. I was rough with the kids and impolite with Madame. I am finally reacting to the shock of Emile's arrest, and my emotions gave way. When one gets so upset, one realizes many things.

I apologized to Madame Grosfils for being rude. I knew at the time that I was rude, but I could not have changed my behavior. I am still a big kid, or perhaps I am not always in control.

♦

My darling, I would so much like to become perfect. I try so hard to become orderly and organized, and it is so difficult!

Yesterday I visited your mother. I never saw anyone so desperate. Nothing in life equals the pain of a mother losing her son.

Parents love their children much more than children love their parents. At the very least, they do not expect their children to die before they do.

My sweet, I am wondering whether you joining the resistance was the right thing to do? It caused such havoc, so much suffering. A family unit is even more selfish than an individual person.

Nelly is pregnant.

♦

Gina and especially Jeanne are becoming increasingly nasty. They are unpleasant whenever I enter the kitchen. I am too friendly. Unfortunately, I guess, one must maintain a respectable distance from one's bosses as well as from one's coworkers. I wish that I could behave that way, but I simply cannot. Let them all go to hell!

Mon petit Emile, sleep well.

Some events are too difficult to contemplate. I cannot, for instance, imagine that you are dead, that I'll never see you again. No, it can't be true. When will this nightmare be over?

♦

8/23/44

Paris was liberated by French troops. The Allies decided that General Leclerq, commanding the Free French forces, would actually boot the Germans out of the capital. I wish I were in Paris today.

To celebrate, the Grosfils opened a bottle of champagne and invited us to share it. Jeanne cried. I think that she faked the tears,

but she impressed Madame Grosfils. Gina is mad at me. The
champagne was delicious.

It is unbelievable how quickly the war now turns in our favor. It
is the end. Let's hope that it is not too late for many of us.

The speed at which news travel also boggles the mind. Ten
minutes after Paris fell, we knew it here in Brussels. The Allies
also liberated Bordeaux and Grenoble in the south of France. I am
reviewing my French geography.

Tonight the Grosfils gave a bridge party. Monsieur and Madame B, people from whom I want to keep my hiding place a
secret, arrived early. I hope that they did not see me. I am not
making much progress with mending Marie's socks.

I am still reading Malraux's "Hope," but am almost finished. I
love certain passages, for example:

"It is not when your friends are right that they need you,
but when they are wrong."

♦

8/24/44

I played volleyball tonight. It was great and made me forget
everything. When I came back home from such an outing I am at
peace with the entire world. Soon I will no longer be excluded from
such ordinary fun.

Two weeks later Nelly called. She said that she had a severe kidney infection and asked whether I would take care of her and Lucette on my day off.
I was proud and grateful that she wanted me to come.

During that visit she told me that Emile had been trapped, ambushed,
and killed by the pro-German militia.

Emile, using the names of Georges and Janssens, had been a commander
of Les Partisans Armés, operating out of Namur. His group carried out
important sabotage operations. Rumor had it that he was betrayed by René,
a double agent and his second in command. Since René, in turn, was shot
by the Gestapo six weeks later, Emile's death was never quite resolved.

I did not know what to say to Nelly. There was my own secret love.
Imaginary at it was, it had sustained me these past two years, and my loss
was real. There was the immense pain I felt for my friends, who had helped

save my life and shape the adult I wanted to be. It was the first time I had to deal with the finality of the death of someone I cared for deeply.

Back home at the Grosfils', I wrote Nelly a letter which I never sent:

8/27/44

Chere Madame [Nelly]:

I am glad that your kidney infection is over and that you feel better. I hope that your baby will continue to behave itself until it is born. I enjoyed playing with Lucette and helping you out last week.

The news of Emile's death crushed me. This war destroys the best among us. Selfish people, who do not take chances, usually escape. The saddest part about Emile's death is that it happened so near the end. Another "five minutes" and he would have been safe.

I hope that the baby you carry is a boy. Perhaps, in some small way, he will replace the son your mother lost. How is my Lucette? Have her tonsils already been removed?

Say hello to your mother for me, and please accept my sympathy. I hope that all these sacrifices will not have been in vain.

♦

8/31/44

One must never believe in anything.

As the Allies approached Brussels, the Germans and their fellow travelers packed up and departed for Germany. For days a weird assemblage of vehicles stuffed with furniture and topped off by mattresses passed our house. The citizens of Brussels could not suppress their glee. All major thoroughfares were lined with spectators.

9/4/44

The German exit from Brussels was comic. During the two days preceding their final retreat, the German army, or what is left of it, continuously tramped by our house on the Avenue de Tervuren.

It was quite a spectacle. The Germans sold everything: sugar, bicycles, watches, automobile parts, binoculars. A horse and cart cost 1,000 francs, a machine gun 260 francs. The Belgian Fascists left too. They were crammed into crowded trucks as if they were beasts. Monsieur Grosfils snapped a photograph of a particularly pathetic-looking German soldier. When he noticed it, the soldier asked Monsieur Grosfils to hand him the film. Fortunately he did not insist on having the camera.

When the fall of Brussels was imminent, my mother called me at the Grosfils' and told me to come home. Since they had been so kind to me I really did not want to leave them, especially without giving official notice. I felt, however, that I could not disobey my mother. I left on the afternoon of September 3.

9/4/44

Since there were no streetcars I had to walk all the way to my mom's house [a distance of about three miles]. I saw the last German soldier at the Chasse [a major intersection]. People were busy looting the German merchandise depots and abandoned trucks. Depending on the depot, one could get meat, bread, and lots of wine and liquor. Unfortunately, I only passed a depot storing household goods. I came home with five mugs, seven glasses, three brushes, and one sieve.

After I got home, I wanted to leave immediately to welcome the British tanks that rattled along the nearby Avenue Louise. A lifetime ago, in May 1940, I had been there when the Allies poured into Belgium to protect us from the Germans. I had seen them leave three weeks later in La Panne, when we too tried to escape from the clutches of the Nazis. Now after millions of civilians and soldiers had perished, the British were back.

My mother, fearing snipers, did not let me go. Perhaps she was right, but I had dreamt so much of this moment that I resented remaining imprisoned behind closed, blacked-out windows. I thought of Emile and all the others, known and unknown, who had died. I thought of how difficult it would be to pick up the pieces. I knew that someday soon I would have to leave the little country that I grew to love and go to America. Since I was no longer living with strangers, I did not have to control my feelings, and I cried my eyes out.

◆

The next morning when I got up, the Belgian flag flew over the radio station, Place de la Croix.

I left the house and took my first stroll through liberated Brussels. I saw the first British soldiers since they left us in La Panne four years earlier. People sacked and looted the homes of the Rexists. They deserve it, but it still is a disgusting sight. All their belongings are thrown out of the window: china, furniture, bedding, papers. Then the pile of junk is ignited. At one house the smoke was so thick that the fire department had to put the fire out. The crowd cheered.

I saw a parade headed by an upside-down portrait of Hitler wearing a Rexist cap and carrying a Negro baby doll.

The Front Independant came out of the woodwork and is all over the place. How young most of its members are. For the first time in my life I saw the insignia of the Communist Party. However, there were very few Red flags. How unfair. I will keep the faith.

During the afternoon I flirted with two British soldiers. On the Avenue Louise, I climbed aboard some British tanks. I conducted an impromptu concert. I boarded a British truck and crisscrossed town, talking to some Irish soldiers. I enjoyed myself tremendously.

I was overjoyed to meet a group with arm bands saying: "Liberated Jews." I spoke to a Belgian soldier. Finally I found a friendly British airman who lives thirty kilometers from Nottingham. I asked him to write to my grandmother and aunt whose address I remembered. I returned home via streetcar, and now I am ready for bed.

If I could forget about you, Emile, this would have been the most beautiful day of my life. As it is, I much prefer the evening we spent on the terrace in Auderghem. My love, I need you so much.

The airman from Nottingham indeed wrote to my family via military mail. Within a week or so my aunt received the following letter:

Dear Mrs. Wertheimer [my Aunt Erna],

Please allow me to introduce myself. I am an airman serving in

France and have recently been in Belgium, where I met your grand-
daughter, Suzanne Bamberger of 34 Avenue de la Cascade. She and
her mother and sister are very well and send you their heartiest
greetings—this is the message she gave me personally and I promised that I would correspond with you and convey their greetings.
It may surprise you to know that I live in Nottingham also, and I
sincerely hope that I have the pleasure of your acquaintance at
some future date.

Well there is little else I can tell you in this letter, I feel my
intentions have been accomplished but I assure you that here in
Belgium everyone is extremely happy, and the distress that has
been done in the past is being cleaned by the military and civil
administration.

So you can be happy in the knowledge that all is well; you have
no need to worry. Just for now I will close with my best wishes and
I shall look forward to your letter.

I remain yours kindly,
Frank Bramwell, RAF

My grandmother cabled the good news to my anxious father in New York.

9/5/44

Life continues and I participate in the general elation of being
rid of the Germans. I am turning into a disgusting flirt. Though I
don't approve, I am quite good at flirting, and am becoming less of
a romantic.

I drank a glass of beer with a British soldier and a martini with
two young, charming Belgian lawyers. They complained that all
the women run after soldiers, neglecting common male mortals
like themselves.

I finally had my first kiss on the mouth. It was a terrible letdown. I believed that kissing was something magic. My first kiss
left me cold and disappointed.

I smoke a lot and I have a big cold. I have fun, but find it
superficial. One must, however, adapt to the circumstances. I am
learning English. I hope that the soldiers will stay here for at least
a month, so I can continue to get cheap lessons.

Emile, I will visit Nelly. I'll probably again behave more responsibly after that.

I went to see whether Elizabeth and the Hollenders returned to their house. As yet nobody was there, but the neighbors said they will be home soon.

On the Avenue Louise, I saw German prisoners. Seeing them felt strange.

I am not very proud of myself.

♦

9/8/44

Emile, yesterday I visited your sister. To me she seems very different. She is sad and depressed, but does not say much.
I know no one else quite like her. She still intimidates me so much that I stutter when I talk to her.

I went to the office of the Friends of the Soviet Union and was impressed. If you were alive, you might be there holding court.
I still regret that I did not manage to join the resistance. I'll never forgive myself.

I went back and visited the Grosfils. The kids screamed with joy when I arrived. Madame Grosfils told me that I really understood the character of each child so perfectly that I contributed to their growth as individuals. Well, perhaps there are some things that I do well.

On the way home I met a young man who asked me for a date. I agreed to tomorrow afternoon. Perhaps I'll go; he looked nice.

In the evening the De Backers came over to visit us. They are our first post-occupation guests. I enjoyed chatting with [their daughter] Eva.

Emile, why did they kill you at the last minute? Now everything is over. I wish that I believed in God. Then I could imagine that your soul survived and that you now glory in Heaven.

Willy, Suzy's fiance, also got caught and killed. I made a condolence call to his mother. It was most painful—there should be a law against mothers losing their children.

♦

9/10/44

LET US NOT FORGET.

So many people think that one simply can forget what happened and return to the past.

I am afraid to forget; afraid not to be able to remember the suffering, the uncertainty, and the fear. I am afraid the world will return to the hum-drum ways that existed before the war, afraid that it will let events slide until a catastrophe becomes inevitable.

I do not want to forget those who died at the front, the deported, the assassinated.

I hope that they did not die in vain, and that we will avenge them by continuing their battles.

I hope we can keep the world at peace.

I recontacted some of my prewar friends. Hedi is very depressed and Inge is a boy-crazy fool.

Very soon after the liberation, I sought out the hastily opened quarters of L'Armée Belges des Partisans. This was the resistance group with whom Emile had fought. I felt bad about joining now, after the fact, and sharing in their glory. They could use clerical help, however, and it made me feel closer to my beloved.

One evening in September our doorbell rang. We had not gotten over the fear of unexpected visitors, especially late at night and were wary when we saw two men. One was our downstairs neighbor from our old apartment in Forest. He had stored some of our belongings when we went into hiding, and at first had been reluctant to return them to us. We wondered whether he had devised some act of revenge. Actually, he simply accompanied my cousin Gerald Bamberger, now a sergeant in the American army, who had tried to find us at our last legal address.

My U.S. soldier cousin Gerald Bamberger showed up one night. He was overjoyed at us being alive. He stayed for three days relishing the bed in Mrs. Lebacqz's little garret. My mom gave him a pair of pajamas retrieved from Herbert Sterner's old suitcase. Jerry reveled in this luxury. This war is hard on all of us. I detested everything Jerry told me about New York.

The idea of again having a father and an extended family seemed strange. We had not heard from my father for more than three years, and the prospect of joining him in America was distasteful. I was barely learning to navigate again in the normal outside world and did not want to know that my adjustment was temporary only.

Not having a son of his own, my father had always dearly loved this nephew, and now Jerry was taking good care of us. He managed to buy us military rations, and all of a sudden we had some extra food. This was fortunate. Out of respect for Belgium's liberation, the black market had crumbled, even though our food supply had dwindled some more. So we were hungrier during the fifth winter of the war than before.

With Jerry's help we now corresponded regularly with Vati. My parents must have argued about Miss Botmann and our move to the United States. My mother shared only a few of these letters. I did not mind; I was so busy sorting out my own life. Even my trusty diary had outlived its usefulness.

◆

10/12/44

A whole month has passed without my making any entries. Since then we had six weeks of freedom. Only six weeks—to me they seem an eternity.

I joined the office of the partisans as a volunteer secretary and am working hard. Mon chèri, I am getting to know your young, handsome, and dedicated friends.

I am very depressed; I feel as if I can't go on. I know, however, from living with myself, that in a couple of days I'll feel better. I am dead tired. I again went to visit your family in Scheut, and when I come back I can't sleep.

Tomorrow they'll bury you. I'll probably go, though I still am not sure whether I'll be strong enough.

I knew from Nelly that Emile's remains would be transferred from a temporary grave to the family plot in the Cemetery of Anderlecht. I reported this to the commander at the partisan headquarters, and he hastily arranged a military funeral.

◆

The partisans will be represented at your funeral. I told them about it and they decided to trot out the big guns. Arranging for this honor guard is probably the only thing that I ever really did for you. Actually I don't care about funerals. I believe that you too would not care, because once one is dead, one is dead.

I seldom felt as abandoned and as lonely as now. I hope that I'll find something useful to do with my life. In spite of that, I wish that each day had at least 48 hours. Perhaps then I would have time to straighten myself out.

At home things are not good. I do not get along with my mother. During the past two years I missed tenderness—and now that I am back home it is still missing. I withdraw more and more. I am so torn between two worlds, two duties, two desires.

When we were liberated, I was numb and indifferent to my surroundings. Now I care; but, looking back, I think that the indifference was better than the depression that I am struggling with now.

I fear that I am really starting to dislike people. During the past six weeks I have not been alone, and yet there is no one to whom I can talk. And then I think of Emile and the love that never was.

◆

10/13/44

Emile, I did go to your funeral. I cannot believe that you are dead. For me you continue to live. There were several eulogies— one given by the executive of the Establissement Wanner [the Altorfers' family business]. His speech was so atrocious that I would gladly have pushed him into your grave. When my time comes, I do not want a formal funeral.

There were many flowers, one wreath read: FOR MY HUSBAND. Somebody must have bought it for Mariette. Poor woman. Nobody knows whether she is alive or where she is, and she does not know that you are dead.

I am not sure that "our" new social order should start now. We are not ready. The young must first alter their priorities.

Sleep well, mon chèri. From now on you will not have to fight.

◆

This was the last letter to Emile Altorfer:

10/31/44

Emile, mon petit chou, I reread all my scribblings, especially the passages that concern you. I reproached myself again and again that I could not join your fight.

If only you had known how much I loved you. I worship everybody who knew you. I love you more and more. Sunday I went to a rally for Jacquemotte [a left-wing politician]. What a pity that you were not there. Today I ate at "home," that is, the headquarters of the partisans.

I felt like an impostor since I was not in "active combat."

I kiss you, my beloved. Good night.

Epilogue

Looking back at the months and years that followed my illegal existence, I note the vigor with which I repressed the memory of what had happened to me. I made many new friends. I talked little of the previous years, because recollecting them was frightening and I felt most people would not understand my experiences. I am not sure that I ever understood them myself. The Holocaust and its horror remain outside human comprehension. For years I was terrified when I had to speak German to strangers. I rarely volunteered that I was Jewish, though I was most grateful to anyone who asked: "Are you all right? Did your family make it?" These questions were always posed by fellow survivors, and to this day I am most comfortable with those who endured my special kind of nightmare. I did not look at my diary for almost forty years. Perhaps I could not revisit my youth until then.

The liberation, which had come upon all of us so abruptly, left me breathless. All of a sudden I had choices.

October 1944

I have to try to go on and decide what to do.

Should I work with children or adolescents? Should I study
chemistry as I had resolved so long ago? Where do I want to
study? At the Institut Meurice Chimie, which seems easier, or
at the Free University of Brussels, as I dreamt during the occupation? Should I do something entirely different? Currently, none of
this seems to matter much, but I wish that I had a goal.

Half of me was amazingly goal-oriented and trying to dismiss the past
four years as an inconvenient delay. My other half wanted to hang on to
what I had learned about love, hate, courage, and loss.

I had grown up unevenly. In some ways I was older and wiser than my
years. In others, I was much younger than nineteen. Even though I desperately wanted to be like everybody else, I had forgotten how to play and to
talk to my peers.

Sadness—my own and that of my friends—accompanied many of my
pleasures. The war was not over yet. Soldiers and civilians continued to be
killed all over the world. We still did not know what had happened to those
the Nazis had torn from our midst: Pitt, Elizabeth's parents, Mariette,
Joseph Vincke, and millions more.

It was difficult to live at home again. I had been responsible for myself
for two long and difficult years. I did not take kindly to my mother telling
me when to come home, or whom I could or could not date. The very last
entry of my diary refers to that struggle:

11/8/44

My mother has a tyrannical trait and home is turning into a
dictatorship. Resistance, however, is strong!

My top priority was to get on with my studies. When the schools
reopened in November, I felt much too old to return to the lyceé. A special
regulation allowed war victims to attend a university-level institution without finishing their secondary education and take a high-school equivalency
examination at the end of the first year. I hesitated between enrolling in
social-work school or studying chemistry. The latter won out, for several

poor reasons. One was that I owed it to my father to try to take over the family business.

I registered at the Institut Meurice Chimie to study chemistry. I was of course totally unprepared for the school, but I worked extremely hard and managed to finish the first year with "distinction."

The professors who gave the equivalency test in the fall of 1945 were kind and forgiving. I was not afraid of the liberal arts portion of the exam, but I knew that my math was very shaky. Luck would have it that I pulled the one question I knew the answer to: the Pythagorean theorem governing the interrelationship of the sides of a right-angled triangle. I passed.

I reveled in the realization that I was attractive and that men could fall in love with me. I collected boys by the carload. I fell in love often, but never with the right guy. Either they loved someone else, or I found them physically attractive and intellectually repulsive, or the other way around. Whenever dates turned serious, I said that I could not get deeply involved, because I was about to leave for the United States. My many encounters were limited to hot kisses and necking. This was accepted behavior for girls. The boys of my school openly visited brothels. In spite of all that playing around, I established some loyal, long-lasting friendships.

Senseless, illogical bureaucracy again interfered with my newly won freedom. Within weeks after the Germans left, the Belgian government-in-exile returned. One of its first acts was to arrest enemy aliens. Since we were again German nationals, we were slated to be detained in a camp. The American Joint Committee intervened in behalf of German Jewish survivors of the war. Our good friends the De Backers and Nelly provided us with testimonials that "we were and had always been loyal to the Belgian nation." We escaped actual imprisonment. Instead we were on probation and had to report once a week to the police stations. Having survived four years of German occupation and considering myself a very loyal Belgian, I found these visits to the police station galling and humiliating.

By June 1944 the Germans had perfected their "secret weapons"—two types of unmanned missiles called V-1 and V-2. The *V* stood for "Vergeltung," which means *reprisal* in German. The missiles were aimed at Britain or Antwerp, the Belgian deep-sea port where most of the supplies for Western

Europe were unloaded. A number of rockets did not reach their target, and some fell on Brussels.

I had joined a Red Cross unit, which was called upon during various emergencies. Assisting at disaster sites was one of our tasks. The unit was summoned when a German missile dropped on "My Children," one of Brussels's boarding schools. Fortunately, the missile hit the school on a weekend, when most of the children had gone home.

We were assigned the task of sifting through the rubble to locate possible survivors. It was a grim chore. After a while we found the bodies of the two headmistresses. I almost became sick looking at the two old women. With determination and black humor, my companions and I managed to press on with our gory search.

An hour later we found a child, aged about ten. Her smiling, relaxed face, framed by long, entangled hair, made me think that she was simply sleeping. She was dead. The reason for her being at My Children on Sunday was that she had no home. She was a Jewish orphan. Her parents had been caught and deported to Poland. By now they had presumably been gassed. A kind uncle had been paying the little girl's tuition. I went home, as the sun was rising over Brussels, despondent over the futility and capriciousness of life.

We thought that we had gotten rid of the Germans for good. But on December 16, 1944, in the middle of winter, Hitler launched a surprise attack in the Ardennes, the Belgian mountain chain near the German border. For this, their last effort, the Germans mustered a quarter of a million men and eleven hundred tanks. Their goal was to slow the Allied advances and to secure Antwerp. At first the so-called Battle of the Bulge was a success for the crumbling Third Reich.

Belgium is a very small country. Though the Battle of the Bulge never threatened the ultimate outcome of World War II, there was a distinct possibility that part of Belgium, including Brussels, would be overrun. All those who had lived underground, and those who had given them shelter, were petrified at the thought of the Germans returning. All of us had bragged about how we had managed to survive the occupation and we would have no place to hide. Christmas 1944 was bleak.

The Allied commanders and their valiant men managed to contain the advance. By January 26, the last German hurrah was over, but seventy-seven thousand Allied soldiers were dead.

♦

Two months after Jerry Bamberger had come to see us, our doorbell rang again. It was Ernest Worth (Wertheimer), the son of my aunt Erna. I had loved him as a child. When I had been eight years old, I had resolved to marry him when the time came. Ernest was in the British Pioneer Corps. Since he had family in Brussels, his commander let him transfer to the Belgian capital. Soon thereafter, a third cousin, Rudy Bamberger, also in the American army, showed up. It was strange and wonderful to renew these long-lost bonds with my far-flung family. My cousins were almost as happy to have a home-away-from-home as we were to have them. Nobody, in Brussels, of course, believed that these attractive young men were my real cousins, and explanations to my admirers were pointless.

On one of my expeditions downtown I met my old friend Gina, the chambermaid from the Grosfils' house. She wore elegant clothes and looked happy as she was waiting for her current date, an American soldier. I hoped that he was serious about her, but somehow I doubted it.

The war in Europe ended on May 8, 1945. All of Brussels, but especially the British, American, and Canadian soldiers, started an endless series of celebrations. I wish that I could report that I too was overjoyed, but the stress of all that had happened weighed me down.

Trains full of the remnants of Hitler's camps started pouring through Brussels. My Red Cross unit was on hand to distribute coffee, soup, and other small kindnesses. The military prisoners usually were in fair shape, the civilians not. Pitt returned from Oranienburg, a German forced-labor camp. He was emaciated but recovered his health quickly. We continued to be good friends; sometimes, when Pitt had money, we went out in grand style.

Mariette Altorfer also survived her incarceration. From Brussels, the Germans had deported her to various fortresses and slave-labor camps in Eastern Europe. There she formed close bonds with two other Belgian prisoners. In 1945, when these camps were about to be overtaken by the Russians, the Nazis marched their freezing, half-starved prisoners toward Germany. Mariette and her friends escaped, slowly making their way toward the Allied lines. Before being repatriated, she sent a cable to Emile. Upon her return to Brussels, she learned that he was no more. When she had somewhat recovered, she sent for Annie and resumed her teaching job. She

never remarried and during her long life never lost faith in her—and Emile's—
Communist ideals.

I had of course never become a "true Communist." Eventually, many of
the people and writers that I had admired while growing up also abandoned
"the God That Failed." Uprooting and cross-cultural breeding had made me
independent and solitary. I belonged everywhere and nowhere. During my
entire life I never truly adhered to any one particular group or organization.

Elizabeth was as much in a hurry to get on with her life as I was. After
she returned to Brussels from her country exile, she submerged herself in
leftist politics and started nurse's training. Her time was at a premium, and
we drifted apart.

Like tens of thousands of others, Elizabeth started searching for her
parents. For a while she hoped against hope that at least one of them had
survived. This was not the case; both had perished in a German extermination camp, as had the Hollenders' eldest daughter, her husband, and her six-
year-old son. The Hollenders continued to treat Elizabeth as their own,
beloved child.

The loss of my friend saddened me. Since my family remained intact, I
attributed the end of our friendship to the fact that for Elizabeth I was a
constant reminder of her own tragedy.

In 1954 Elizabeth got married to a Belgian doctor and moved to Mons,
a small Belgian mining town where both she and her husband practiced.
Elizabeth had three children, two almost the exact age of mine. When I
visited her in 1964, she was happy and at peace.

Because we were the wife and minor children of an American resident,
our American visas were issued rather rapidly. For weeks I said good-bye to
the many who had helped save my life: the De Backers, the Wiames, the
Grosfils, Fuss, Suzy the milliner, and the teachers at my school. Tante Bets
was sad and subdued. Her beloved brother, his wife, and their five children
had indeed perished in the Holocaust.

On May 11, 1946, my mother, sister, and I left Brussels by plane—as we
had arrived eight years earlier. Harry Salomon and a few of my beaux
escorted us to the airport. I was heartbroken that I had to leave the little
country that had sheltered me from Nazis and the friends I made before,

during, and after the war. I knew it would take me a long time to become proficient enough in yet another language to make my new country truly "mine." It would take even longer to grow roots once more.

Of the four of us, the war had been hardest on my father. Though he was only fifty-eight when he met our ship in New York harbor, he seemed to be an old man. Family and friends tell me that during the entire war, he lived in a constant state of anxiety. Yet, in 1941, shortly after he arrived in New York, he had founded yet another small chemical plant. He christened it Chemo-Puro. It prospered because, at the time, the supply of fine chemicals from Germany had come to a halt.

During my first New York summer, I worked as my father's laboratory assistant, as I had planned so long ago. Fate would have it that I never actually helped him run his business.

My cousin Herbert Sterner was still imprisoned in Gurs at the time my father had been released from their common concentration camp in southern France. Fortunately, Herbert escaped thereafter, shortly before all the inmates were shipped to Poland. Herbert managed to reach Switzerland. The news of his survival lifted a great burden from my mother's shoulders. Herbert had written that he thought of my mother often and could keenly "hear" her disapproval when he was excessively messy. It was his way of thanking my mother for getting him out of Germany.

Herbert contacted us once more when we were in New York. By then he had married his pregnant Swiss sweetheart. The two were on their way to Venezuela, where Herbert allegedly had a very rich, childless relative. When Herbert's South America–bound ship docked in New York, my parents went to see him, delivering the suitcase he had left with us in Brussels so many years earlier. Herbert's parents and grandmother had perished, and the suitcase contained a few reminders from the home he had been so attached to.

Though our move to America again interrupted my studies, I was determined to finish my education. At twenty-one, I felt much too old to go to college. Tenacious, but unrealistic, I talked my way into Columbia University's graduate school. Eventually my nonexistent mathematics background took its toll, and I never quite finished my master's degree in chemistry. I qualified for employment as a laboratory technician and worked at Sloan-Kettering Institute for Cancer Research, and then at New York

University. Not completing my education, as I had resolved to do so long ago, however, left me with a profound sense of failure.

As soon as we had arrived in America, my parents bought a small house in Forest Hills. We had great trouble functioning again as a family. There was much yelling and dissent, which increased when my widowed, by-now slightly senile, grandmother, joined us in 1947.

Even though it all seemed to have taken place in another life, our German past started to reemerge. It so happened that the German lawyer who dealt with my father's restitution claim against the Chemical Factory Lehrte had been a classmate of mine in Hanover. Hans Pessler associated the name of the former owner of the property he was handling with that of the child who had given him foreign stamps for his stamp collection. When we had established that I indeed was that child, I started receiving letters from Germany. Three of my former classmates had been killed on the Russian Front. Others had lost their homes. The war had been hard, but by now most everybody had resumed their normal day-to-day existence. None of the letters mentioned the havoc the war had caused throughout the world. Worst of all, nobody mentioned Ruth-Iris, who had perished in a death camp. I had not liked Ruth-Iris all that much, but of all the victims of the Holocaust, her death, which so nearly could have been mine, touched me most personally.

Even Miss Botmann resurfaced. Apparently she and my father had resumed their secret correspondence. Vati kept her supplied with nylons, food, and other necessities!

I had never forgotten the address of Marie, the woman who had been living with my parents when I was born. I dropped her a note. Her answer, showing her unabashed joy that I still existed, was the only missive from Germany I cherished.

Gaby and I felt extremely responsible for our parents relationship, taking our father to the movies and our mother on walks. Laughingly, our parents reassured us that they were getting along quite well when they were on their own. Eventually there was indeed less fighting. In May 1949 we celebrated my parents' silver wedding anniversary. Six months later my father died unexpectedly, three and a half years after we had been reunited.

My mother was only forty-eight years old at the time. My father left her enough money to live in relative comfort for another forty years. She never remarried, nor worked, but was quite content. For her, the years we had spent in Belgium, escaping the Holocaust, remained the most meaningful ones of her entire life. Her best friend during the long evening of her life was Mrs. Beissinger, whose husband had been imprisoned with my father in the south of France. In 1941, the Beissingers had left Brussels for unoccupied France. From there, they went to Spain, then Cuba, and they arrived in New York in 1946.

Nelly and I slowly became—and remained—good friends. I felt brave when I started calling her simply by her first name, instead of addressing her as "Madame Nelly." In 1948, she visited me in New York. Actually, she was on her way to Washington University in Saint Louis, where Jean held a post-doctoral fellowship. By the time Nelly joined him, however, Jean had already fallen in love with another woman. So ended what I had viewed as a magic marriage.

Nelly bore this loss with her usual courage and stoicism, conscientiously bringing up Lucette and Jacques, the little boy born just after the end of the occupation. Whenever I visited Brussels, I stayed with Nelly. Though I had actually lived with the Wiames for only eight months, Nelly's house, with its many books, pictures, zoological and botanical artifacts, and family photographs always made me feel that I was coming home. Emile's photograph stood prominently on the buffet in the living room. How young his thirty years now looked to my fifty. In the bedroom, Nelly kept a photograph of Lucette and baby Jacques. Did anyone remember that I had taken that picture before I left for America?

I loved my visits to Brussels. I checked on my many friends. Madame Lebacqz, we learned, eventually joined her son in California, but she died shortly after she had arrived in America. Her son wrote to us, telling us how much she had loved us all. The Bellins, who had rented a room to my mother at the beginning of our illegal existence, had applied to the proper authorities and were decorated for having helped us survive. Harry Salomon had died, but Gretel always invited me to an elegant lunch. It was accompanied by fantastic wines now selected by Martin, who had taken over the family business. Pappy Hirschland also died, but Alma, Gert, Pitt, and Dédé, their spouses, and children were happy to see me.

I spent time with the friends I had made during my student days, but most of all I enjoyed walking around the streets of Brussels, soaking up the French, the smells, the clanking of the streetcars, and recapturing some of the dreams of my youth.

Nelly died in 1979. For me, her sudden, untimely death, which almost coincided with one of my visits to her, broke one of the remaining links to what I like to think of as my hometown. I still keep up with Lucette and Jacques and their family, and they welcome me warmly whenever I come to Brussels.

At Columbia, I had met Ernest M. Loebl, a doctoral student in chemistry. He had been born in Vienna, and his family had fled to Palestine, the future Israel. He had not actually gone through the Holocaust. The magnitude of catastrophe that had befallen his people, however, cast a permanent shadow on how he perceived life. Ernest and I were married in March 1950. After he graduated, he became a professor at the Polytechnic Institute of Brooklyn. We continued to live in New York, a city in whose multiethnic, multinational atmosphere we eventually again felt at home.

Ernest and I made many friends, most of whom were intellectuals. Our social life, with its little dinner parties and interesting conversations, was what I had dreamt of when I was at the Wiames'. Judy, our daughter, was born in 1954. For a very short while I called her Lucette, and burped her in French. When David was born in 1956, my little family was a replica of Nelly's.

Even though I was much happier than I had dared to hope for during my adolescence, I was humiliated by not having what I considered to be a respectable career. I had made getting an education in spite of all the obstacles that were in my path a personal battle between me and my by-now mercifully absent Nazi tormentors. Being at home, taking care of my young children, forced me to reflect.

I realized by then that I never would be a great chemist, but I wanted to make use of my very solid scientific education. I had always loved to write; was fluent in English, French, and German; and had never forgotten the excitement I felt during Mademoiselle Feytmans's history lessons. Timidly, almost by accident, I combined my scientific training with my other assets and became a science writer. My first book, dealing with the discovery of viruses and vaccines, was published in 1967. In 1968, the School of Journalism at Columbia University awarded me a fellowship in advanced science writing and granted me a degree. I found work, wrote a few books, and was fulfilled. Thus ended my personal quest for a meaningful career.

My sister also managed to put the Holocaust behind her. She always was a better student than I. She came to America speaking English flawlessly, entered the senior year at Forest Hills High, went on to Queens College, graduated in 1950, and obtained a doctorate in French literature from Yale University. Columbia University, which played such an important role in my life, also provided her with a husband. In 1957, she married Victor Lewinson, one of my husband's fellow graduate students.

I have never regretted growing up at the edge of the Holocaust. It made me a stronger, more compassionate human being. And strange as it might sound, the experience provided me with a deep faith in humanity. Though there is much evidence to the contrary, I believe that when you have your back against the wall, somebody out there may come to the rescue.

But I know how lucky I was. My family escaped intact, and most of my other relatives also managed to reach safety.

I well remember the fears, the nightmares, the deaths of loved ones, the loneliness, the helplessness, and being at the mercy of strangers and informers. I still feel the extreme frustration of being powerless in the face of mortal danger. Yet I did not have to witness the horrors of the camps; the trip to the gas chamber; share the long death marches; or suffer from extreme cold, hunger, or illness. I did not have to steal bread from my dying parent or make other inhuman decisions that forever after would have haunted my days and nights.